THE LIBRARY OF EDUCATIONAL THOUGHT

Edited by C. H. Dobinson

PESTALOZZI

J.H. PESTALOZZI at the age of about 60
(from a drawing attributed, probably incorrectly, to F.M. Diogg)

PESTALOZZI

His thought and its relevance today

MICHAEL HEAFFORD

METHUEN & CO LTD
11 NEW FETTER LANE · LONDON EC4

First published 1967 by Methuen & Co Ltd

Printed in Great Britain by
Richard Clay (The Chaucer Press), Ltd, Bungay, Suffolk

Distributed in the U.S.A. by Barnes & Noble, Inc.

Contents

Preface

Pestalozzi – the name probably conjures up the picture of refugee children in one of the Pestalozzi International Children's Villages. The man who gave his name to the villages has almost faded into historical oblivion, at least in English-speaking countries. And yet in his lifetime he was as much a legend as was, for example, Albert Schweitzer in the first half of this century – and he succeeded in arousing the same feelings of admiration and scepticism, devotion and criticism. Young men came from all over Europe to work with Pestalozzi at one of his institutes, while he strove to persuade the doubting rulers of Europe to adopt his method of education; he had audiences with the King of Prussia and the Tsar of Russia, he corresponded with Leopold II before he became Emperor of Austria, and he was a member of a Swiss delegation sent in 1802 to negotiate with Napoleon in Paris. However, it is not merely as a historical figure that Pestalozzi is to be considered here, but as a man whose ideas have been all too often neglected, despite the fact that many of them are as interesting and as relevant as they were when first formulated.

The book opens with a section on Pestalozzi's life, as, to do him justice, it is essential to see him against his historical and personal background. Also, even if our prime consideration is for Pestalozzi's educational ideas, it is necessary to show that he attempted to put these ideas into practice and the circumstances in which he did so.

Pestalozzi was a writer with a vigorous style, and therefore many quotations from his works have been included in the book in the hope that they will reveal some of the energy and enthusiasm with which he expressed his ideas and feelings.

In the second section of the book Pestalozzi's educational ideas are considered. These have often been treated from a historical angle, and their gradual emergence during the course of Pestalozzi's life is shown. Such an approach is valuable if one's purpose is to throw light on Pestalozzi himself and on how his maturing personality and increasing experience made him continually modify his theories. Here the intention is to put forward his ideas in such a way that they are seen to be relevant to many aspects of present-day educational discussion. In part this is done implicity; the very ideas one selects and the way one presents them are necessarily such as should appeal to the modern reader. In the conclusion the explicit attempt has been made to establish links between Pestalozzi's views and certain modern trends in educational theory. The ordered account of Pestalozzi's theories loses something from the historian's and biographer's point of view; in contrast it makes Pestalozzi's ideas more accessible – and herein lies the aim of this small volume.

In conclusion I would like to thank Professor Dobinson for his valuable suggestions throughout the writing of this book. My thanks must also go to the Director of the Pestalozzianum in Zürich, Dr Wymann, who provided much useful information, and who kindly gave permission for the frontispiece portrait to be reproduced and for quotations to be made from Pestalozzi's works under copyright with the Pestalozzianum.

PART ONE

Pestalozzi's Life

1 · The Early Years

Today Zürich is a large and prosperous town, the seat of one of the most famous technological universities in Europe, and a centre of world banking. In the eighteenth century the town was already a commercial and cultural centre. Then, however, unlike today, the wealth of the town was in the hands of a very few families and the rest of the population lived in poverty. The constitution was in theory a democratic one, as all citizens could vote; but for many years it had become impossible to become a citizen – citizenship being passed from father to son like a kind of title. The form of government was, therefore, almost as despotic as that in neighbouring France, with the result that, as the century drew on, there were moves, mainly initiated by liberal-minded but uninfluential citizens, for political and social reforms.

It was in Zürich that Johann Heinrich Pestalozzi was born in 1746, the second of three children.

> From the cradle I was delicate and weakly; from a very early age I distinguished myself in the vigour with which I developed some of my faculties and inclinations; but just as I took a warm interest in certain objects and points of view, I equally showed myself, at just as early an age, extremely inattentive and indifferent to everything which was not in some way actively connected with one of the objects temporarily occupying my fancy.[1]

An examination of Pestalozzi's early life does give some indication of why these personal characteristics should have developed. The Pestalozzi family had moved to Zürich in the sixteenth century and become citizens of the town. Therefore Pestalozzi was born into the privileged section of Zürich society. In contrast, his father had little money and when he died but six years after Pestalozzi's birth, he could only pass on a small inheritance with which to maintain his family. Thus Pestalozzi was brought up with great simplicity and came in contact with the poor far more than most young 'citizens'. The death of his father influenced not only the outward conditions in which he grew up, but also the nature of his upbringing. For there was now only his mother and the family's faithful servant, Barbara Schmid, to look after him. The close relationship between mother and child, which Pestalozzi was to extol later on, became all-important. What Pestalozzi felt to have been lacking was that influence in home life which springs from the father. To the lack of the firm guiding hand of a father Pestalozzi attributed his over-sensitive, even unstable, character.

The family lived in the old part of Zürich in a small house with a single living-room. On occasion, however, Pestalozzi was taken to visit his grandfather in the village of Höngg, just outside Zürich. Here his grandfather was pastor – a pastor who maintained the education of the village children and who cared for the welfare of all his parishioners. The poverty of the villagers, the simplicity of their lives, and the social concern of his grandfather, all influenced Pestalozzi. Later he was to choose a country life rather than remain in Zürich, and would show an even greater concern than his grandfather for the poor, and, above all, for their education.

At school he proved a good pupil – at least in those subjects which interested him. When in 1763 he entered the higher secondary school, called the Collegium Carolinum, he came under the lively influence of such teachers as Bodmer and Breitinger. These two men were, in fact, well known in the German-speaking world of the time, for they were involved in a literary argument over the value of German as a language in comparison with French. At the beginning of the eighteenth century French was regarded as the language of culture throughout Europe and even Frederick the Great of Prussia accused the German language of being as 'barbarous as the Goths and Huns who corrupted it'.[2] So the views held by Bodmer and Breitinger that German could be just as expressive as French and the recommendation that German writers should turn to English works as well as French ones for inspiration were highly controversial. The progressive ideas of some of the Carolinum teachers were not limited to literary matters but spread into the field of politics. In 1762 Bodmer set up a society which was called the 'Helvetische Gesellschaft zu Gerwe'. The members of the society also called themselves 'Patriots' for they urged widespread political and social reform which they believed was for the good of their country. Many of the young men of Zürich, including Pestalozzi, joined the society. Later Pestalozzi looked back on his membership of the group with mixed feelings: he approved of the idealism and enthusiasm of the group, but felt that their aims had been far too impractically formulated to make a real impact.

It was understandable that a young man with radical views on social questions would read avidly any books which seemed to support his views. And thus it was that Pestalozzi came to read Rousseau's *Emile*, which had appeared in 1762. Even though he later called the work 'a highly impractical dream-book'[3] he never denied the profound influence it had on him. Rousseau's idea that a child grows up through definite stages was later taken over by Pestalozzi, as were his dislike of book-learning, and above all his concept of 'natural education'. But it was the impact of the book as a whole and its plea for reform, rather than individual precepts, which filled Pestalozzi with enthusiasm. The following words, to be found in the preface to *Emile*, express Rousseau's challenge to the early eighteenth-century attitude to education:

> We do not know children: with the false ideas we have of them, the further we proceed the more we go astray. The wisest concentrate on that which it is important for grown-ups to know, without considering what children are capable of learning. They are always looking for the man in the child without thinking of what he is before he becomes a man.[4]

It was a challenge which Pestalozzi fully recognized as he read the book:

> I compared the education which I had received in a corner of my mother's living-room and in the school class which I had attended with that which Rousseau claimed and demanded for his Emile. Home education as well as public education everywhere and in all

> classes of society appeared to me to be exactly like a crippled figure which would be able to find a cure for the wretchedness of its existing condition in the fine ideas of Rousseau, and that it was there that it should seek this cure.[5]

It was not only Rousseau's *Emile* which appealed to Pestalozzi; the *Social Contract*, which also appeared in 1762, filled him with similar desires to improve social conditions in Zürich. How he should set about doing this Pestalozzi was not sure. He rejected his initial intention of entering holy orders, toyed with the idea of becoming a lawyer, and finally felt that it was by improving the methods of popular education that he could best fulfil his aims in life. But even having made his decision, he was none too certain how to proceed further:

> I knew the way which I planned to take as little as I knew myself and had no idea where it would lead me. As I was then, I was not able even to imagine it and in blind enthusiasm at my newly adopted plan, I made the decision to devote myself whole-heartedly to agriculture.[6]

There seems little compatibility between agriculture and education, but Pestalozzi did attempt to combine them, as will be seen in the next chapter. Certainly both callings could be regarded as means of helping the poor, which was his life's ambition.

Having decided to study agricultural methods, Pestalozzi went, in 1767, to stay with J. R. Tschiffeli at his experimental farm in order to serve a sort of apprenticeship. Tschiffeli was a Bernese patrician who was interested in increasing the productivity of the land and thereby the well-being of the country population as a whole. On his estate at Kirchberg near Bern he experimented both with plant cultures and with new types of machinery. He finally succeeded in greatly increasing the agricultural value of his land and gained a considerable reputation as an innovator in farming methods. Tschiffeli had, however, little business sense and would have found himself in serious financial difficulties had he not had, in 1770, the good fortune to win first prize in a state lottery. Pestalozzi was unaware of Tschiffeli's financial situation and so, shortly after his stay at Kirchberg, he purchased land near the village of Birr fully believing that he could successfully imitate

Tschiffeli's methods. On his new estate he had a house built for him – the Neuhof (i.e. the New Farm).

Apart from his stay with Tschiffeli, 1767 was an important year in Pestalozzi's life. Among the 'Patriots' had been a young man called Hans Kaspar Bluntschli who was a close friend of Pestalozzi. When he died in 1767 at the age of twenty four Pestalozzi felt his loss deeply. The loss was equally felt by Bluntschli's fiancée, Anna Schulthess. In their grief the two found themselves drawn to each other. Their mutual sympathy developed into affection, their affection into love. After finally overcoming the objections of Anna's parents they married in 1769. The marriage had many tensions and difficulties to face; Pestalozzi had, for instance, to leave his wife with friends while he established his institutes; and their only son was never healthy and died at the early age of thirty-one. However, despite all the problems created by marriage to a man who was careless and above all impetuous, Anna stood by him, and, until her death in 1815, showed herself a faithful companion throughout the troubled times which lay ahead. In the Spring of 1771 they moved into the Neuhof.

Pestalozzi's situation even at this point when he was on the verge of his first educational experiment was far from enviable. Firstly, he was finding difficulty in raising the capital necessary to pay for the land, a difficulty aggravated by his having placed his trust in an unscrupulous agent when purchasing it. The land he had acquired was poor in quality and would need much time, energy, and money spent on it if it were to be improved as Tschiffeli's estate had been. In addition, his wife was in no good health and pregnant. Yet set against all the external obstacles and internal deficiencies with which he was faced, Pestalozzi had one outstanding quality – his sense of mission. Not only now but throughout his life he had supreme confidence in himself. The feeling that he was called upon to serve his country and humanity was genuine, and he accepted it with a mixture of pride and humility:

> I had absolutely nothing in my favour except one deep-rooted purpose, one irrevocable motto: I will, – one belief which no experience could shatter: I can – and an indefinable feeling within me: I must.[7]

B

At the age of twenty-one he had written to Anna:

> I will forget my own life, the tears of my wife, and my children in order to be of service to my fatherland.[8]

The channels into which he directed his energies varied during the course of his life, but from the beginning they were aimed at attaining certain social and humanitarian ideals – above all improving the lot of the poor and underprivileged.

2 · The Neuhof Experiment

The first years spent in the Neuhof were a struggle against financial difficulties. Not only Pestalozzi's wife, but several of her relations too, gave or lent money so that the young couple would not sink too deeply into debt. Despite the critical state of his finances Pestalozzi decided to go ahead with a plan which involved taking poor children into the Neuhof and giving them a simple education. As well as their lessons the children would do a certain amount of work by means of which, Pestalozzi hoped, they would earn their keep. The immediate motives behind his decision, he explained as follows:

> I saw in a poor district the misery of those children who were hired out to the farmers by the municipalities; I saw how the oppressive harshness of self-interest, I might almost say, *condemned* nearly all these children in body and in soul; I saw how many, ailing and without courage and energy, could never grow up with those feelings of humanity, with those powers, which would be beneficial to themselves and to the fatherland.[1]

Pestalozzi realized that the education which these children received, if indeed they received any, was that given either by village schoolmasters who had usually chosen that profession because they were capable of none other, or by parents who, whether they pampered the children or maltreated them, did nothing to adapt them to the place in society they would have to fill. A few charitable institutions for the poor had been opened by rich benefactors, but these could never be successful as they failed to take into account the sort of life a poor child would lead when he came to leave the institution:

> The poor must be educated for poverty and this is the key test by which it can be discovered whether such an institution is really

> a good one. Education of the poor demands a deep and accurate knowledge of the real needs, limitations, and environment of poverty, and detailed knowledge of the probable situation in which they will spend their lives. . . .[2]

To be able to educate the poor it was necessary to experience their way of life:

> The friend of humanity must descend into the lowest hovel of misery and must see the poor man in his gloomy room, his wife in a kitchen full of smoke, and his child, all going about their almost unendurable daily duties. For that is the hovel in which a publicly educated child will some day have to live. . . .[3]

Pestalozzi hoped to combine a basic general education with some vocational education in such a way that the poor child would be able to grow into his station in society and at the same time become a responsible member of it.

The first children arrived in the Neuhof in 1774; in 1776 there were twenty two and by 1778 the numbers had increased to thirty seven. The children were given elementary instruction in reading, writing, and arithmetic, as well as in religion. The boys were also engaged on simple agricultural jobs about the farm and did some weaving, while the girls were occupied with spinning, gardening, and cooking. Pestalozzi soon realized, however, that the task he had undertaken was not as easy as it had appeared. Many of the children had previously lived by begging or had remained inactive at home, and such children did not adapt themselves willingly to the strict routine and discipline which were necessary in a large community. Nor at first were there any signs of gratitude from either the children or the parents. The parents often waited until the children had reached working age or had received new clothes, and then persuaded them to run away from the Neuhof and return home.

As the months went by, the children began to settle down and even to thrive. Already in 1775 Pestalozzi noticed that the children were becoming more cheerful and more healthy and in 1777 he could write enthusiastically:

> It is an indescribable joy to see boys and girls, who had been wretched, growing and thriving, to see peace and satisfaction in

> their faces, to train their hands to work, and to lift their hearts towards their Creator . . .[4]

If Pestalozzi was proving correct in his belief that a simple but regular life would benefit the children, he was wrong in thinking that the work they were doing would pay for their keep. At the end of 1775 he found himself forced to make an appeal to those he felt might be prepared to support his enterprise and in the following years he made further similar appeals. At first the response appears to have been favourable, but few people were prepared to contribute a substantial sum of money year after year. In 1779 Pestalozzi had no alternative but to sell some of the land, and in the following year it became clear that the whole enterprise could not continue. The children had to be sent away and Pestalozzi was left exhausted and depressed in what remained of his property.

Pestalozzi recognized that the necessary ending of the experiment was not the result of the poor quality of the land nor of the lack of support of his friends so much as of himself and of his tendency

> to try and climb to the top rung of the ladder leading to my aims, before I had set my foot firmly on the bottom rung.[5]

If he had been slightly less ambitious in his project – by ensuring that he was financially secure before bringing children to the Neuhof and by starting with a smaller number of children – he might well have avoided the ultimate disappointment of 1780. On the other hand a less ambitious man would never have embarked on the project in the first place. Nor was it a complete failure. Pestalozzi had proved to himself, if not to others, that 'in their foundations'[6] his theories had been correct and the experiment gave him practical experience of organizing an institution and of teaching difficult and undisciplined children. Through this experience he had learnt that a successful education depended on providing a child with security and on giving him genuine affection. These were two principles to which Pestalozzi clung throughout his life.

3 · The Years of Inaction

The failure of Pestalozzi's enterprise resulted in virtually all confidence being lost in him; those who had previously supported him now 'completely and blindly rejected even the smallest shadow of respect for my aims and for my capacity to achieve a single part of them'.[1] Pestalozzi became conscious that even his friends avoided him in the street in order to escape the embarrassment of expressing sympathy which would be of no help, and one friend told him that it was generally felt that he would end his days in a hospital or a lunatic asylum. Pestalozzi, however, remained sure of himself: 'My conviction that basically my aims were correct was never stronger than at that point in time when they were outwardly a complete failure.'[2] His ideals, unfortunately, could not feed his family, and so, reluctantly, he turned to writing as a means of earning his living. He did so 'in the same spirit as I would have combed wigs had I thereby been able to help and comfort my wife and child'.[3] Yet with whatever reluctance he might have taken up writing, he soon found that the activity was one which came easily enough to him. Remaining at the Neuhof, he began to note down his reflections on a few general themes which were close to his heart. Beginning with the question, 'man, in his essence, what is he?', Pestalozzi turned his thoughts to the relationship of God and man, and man and nature. The issues in life which concerned Pestalozzi were already emerging; his writing was sincere and enthusiastic, but his thoughts loosely put together. The work which thus emerged, he entitled *The Evening Hour of a Hermit*, and, thanks to an editor friend, Isaac Iselin, he managed to have it published in a periodical in 1780.

The work was not intended to be a philosophical treatise; indeed, its form excluded such a possibility. But in it Pestalozzi was able to give expression to some of his thoughts on the nature of man and the universe. And whereas class-room education is not consciously a central theme in the work, education in a wider sense is shown to be of supreme importance to the whole of society. The key to man's fulfilment, Pestalozzi claimed, lies within himself and, by restoring the human heart to its natural state of innocence and simplicity, man will find inner peace, regain his faith in God, and through his faith recognize a higher purpose in life. By stating that man could be shown *how* to attain the inner peace necessary to comprehend the world around him, Pestalozzi was, from the start, proclaiming his conviction that, through education, the nature of society could be radically reformed.

It was with another book that Pestalozzi achieved sudden fame as a writer. He was experimenting with a story about village life when he found that 'the story, I know not how, flowed from my pen and developed out of itself without my having formed any plan of it in my head'.[4] The result of this 'inspiration' was Part One of *Lienhard and Gertrud*. The scene of the action was the small village of Bonnal. In Bonnal the villagers were dominated by an unscrupulous bailiff called Hummel. They deserved no better, for the social morality of the village had become corrupt and its people self-seeking and superstitious. However, all was not irrevocably lost, for in the figure of the book's heroine, Gertrud, Virtue found her champion. Gertrud, the mother of seven children, appealed to the Squire, Arner, to save her husband, Lienhard, from the clutches of Hummel. Arner, moved by her appeal, realized that he had a responsibility towards the village, and decided to take an active interest in all the people under his care. Hummel was finally relieved of his duties, and, when he resorted to foul play in his attempt to maintain his position, he was imprisoned. With Hummel no longer in a position to obstruct him, Arner was free to set about restoring order and goodwill in the village.

To the modern reader the characterization may appear oversimplified and the theme too moralizing. However, the novel was written as a popular work and it does succeed in maintaining the reader's interest by its continuous action and its vigorous conversational style. When shown the book, Iselin was delighted:

> In this mode of writing it is without parallel, and the views which it affirms are urgently needed by our age.[5]

Whatever deficiencies the work may seem to have to the modern reader, it was widely acclaimed and read when it first appeared. It helped to restore confidence in Pestalozzi. He even received a gold medal from the Bern Economic Society inscribed 'Civi optimo' ('for a most excellent citizen'), which he ironically translated as 'To the worthless citizen for his worthless book'.

But despite this success, as the years went by Pestalozzi felt increasingly frustrated. It was, after all, not his ambition to become a writer:

> I was not brought up to be a writer. I feel at home when I have a child in my arms, or when a man who feels for humanity stands before me. And then I forget the poor truths fashioned by the pen. . . . For of everything which does not interest me as being indispensable to mankind I am unconcerned and the most ignorant of men.[6]

Nothing characterizes this period in Pestalozzi's life more than his increasing concern with human and social problems. Even with *Lienhard and Gertrud* he was dissatisfied. He felt the book was being interpreted too narrowly: Hummel was the exploiter, but not the originator of the decaying moral life of the Bonnal villagers. The real causes lay deeper and demanded more basic cures than the simple removal of the unscrupulous bailiff. So, to make his standpoint clearer, Pestalozzi wrote *Christoph and Else*, a work in which the characters read *Lienhard and Gertrud* and discuss it. Still hoping that his writings would be eventually appreciated for the right reasons, he added three further parts to *Lienhard and Gertrud* designed to show that only through education could the ills of society be cured. The theoretical approach to the subject, however, prevented a repetition of his initial popular success. Indeed, his writing barely earned him enough to live on. Why then, people began to ask, does he not devote himself solely to novel writing, an art at which he showed so much talent, and moreover achieved such success? But if Pestalozzi sought after success, he was certainly not indifferent to the means by which he might gain it. His aims were practical and not artistic, and he therefore regarded his writings as worthless if they did not challenge existing social attitudes and stimulate educational reform.

Shocked by the attitude of his contemporaries towards young

women who, forced by the pressures of a society intolerant of illegitimate birth, killed their own babies, Pestalozzi was moved to write an essay which he entitled *On Legislation and Infanticide*. It was published in 1783. In it he analysed the mother's motives for such an act of desperation and put forward the view that it was society and not the mother who should shoulder the blame. Pestalozzi was in no way attacking the institution of marriage, but advocating the adoption by society of attitudes of tolerance and forgiveness which would render such acts of violence less likely.

As well as writing books, Pestalozzi corresponded with powerful political figures outside Switzerland in the hope that he could interest them in his ideas. Interest them he did, but he never succeeded in persuading them to take the difficult step from theoretical interest to positive action. When the French Revolution broke out, it appeared that in France, at least, the social changes might well provide the opportunity to establish a system of popular education along the lines Pestalozzi advocated. Indeed, in 1792 he was proclaimed an honorary French citizen by the French Parliament, but the increasing violence and unrest put paid to his hopes of putting his ideas into practice. Pestalozzi could only stand by and watch helplessly.

In 1797 he published a long philosophical work entitled *Investigations into the Course of Nature in the Development of the Human Race*. He tried to deduce the basic motives of human actions and thereby to establish the function of education which must harmonize with, not compete against, the natural instincts and desires of man. Although the work does not concern itself directly with school or home education, it helped Pestalozzi to gain a clear understanding of the aims of education. He himself expressed his purpose as 'essentially a means of becoming clear in my own mind about the development of my pet ideas and of reconciling my natural feelings with my conception of civic rights and of morality'.[7] He felt that having written the work he had clarified his own ideas; his readers, however, did not show any enlightenment or appreciation of the ambitious work.

The striking features of Pestalozzi's writing over these twenty years between 1780 and 1799, are the diversity of its matter and the intensity of its arguments. It is essential to realize that Pestalozzi became an educator as a result not of his educational experiences but of his deep social conscience. Education was not simply a matter of teaching children, but of improving society and enabling every individual to live a full and harmonious life. In 1787 Pestalozzi wrote in a letter:

> From my earliest years the topics of law and the education of the people have been the central interest of my life.[8]

Initially Pestalozzi had hoped to improve the lot of the people through blunt external action – through the political activities of the Zürich 'Patriots' and through the agricultural reforms initiated by Tschiffeli. But as he grew older he became increasingly aware that inner reform through education should parallel external reform and finally he came to regard popular education as a prerequisite to political reform:

> The dream of making men something through politics before they really *are* something, this dream has vanished in me. My only politics now is to make something of men and to make as much of them as possible.[9]

Yet even at this stage of his life, when he was still much concerned with politics as such, Pestalozzi was only too aware that both politics and education are by definition practical occupations. And so it is little wonder that we find his frustration at inaction growing. In 1793 he wrote:

> It is indeed true that the existence of him who bears the interest of humanity within his breast is blessed. But if, as helpless as a lame man by the road, he must spend his life calling to blind passers-by: 'Take me on your shoulders and I will show you the way which you cannot see', and in his whole long life not a single one takes him on his shoulders, then he is to be pitied.[10]

The years that Pestalozzi spent confined to his writing desk in the Neuhof were for him the saddest of his life, the ones where his courage ebbed and he felt death would overtake him before he had even begun to realize his ambitions. But, however depressing it was for him, it enabled him to see education in its wide social, political, and moral contexts. The impossibility of action had forced him to examine thoroughly his theories and their implications as well as his own capacities. Later in life, having been given the opportunity to practise as well as to preach, he willingly recognized how essential to his own development had been his frustrations and disappointments:

> The sufferings of my life were of more value to me than ever its enjoyments can be. The sufferings of my life made that mature in me which would never have matured if I had been happy.[11]

Finally, in 1799, came the first opportunity to prove that the years of inactivity had not been spent in worthless dreaming.

4 · Stans

Since the outbreak of the French Revolution in 1789, the political situation in Switzerland had not been stable. There had been hopes that the upper classes might renounce their privileges and establish a more democratic constitution. The brutalities which occurred in the wake of the initial enthusiasm and idealism in France naturally dampened Swiss desires to emulate the French. The Swiss were, however, given little choice in the matter. All opposition to the Revolution having been finally stamped out in France, the French turned to consolidating their new regime abroad by military means. A desire to spread their new political ideas, along with the practical motive of ensuring a free passage for their troops to Italy, led them, in 1798, to attack and defeat the Bernese. The Swiss Confederation (which consisted of some dozen cantons, including Bern) offered no further resistance and the French were left free to replace it by a new federal government. Understandably the new government was viewed with mixed feelings by the population. It abolished many of the abuses which had existed under the old regime, but had to contend with the unpopularity of a government set up by a foreign power.

Pestalozzi's reactions to the Revolution were similar to those of many of his compatriots. While earnestly desiring political change and admiring many of the humanitarian ideals of the revolutionaries, he naturally disapproved of the means they adopted to gain their ends. His belief in the need for educating the common people was hardened. If only the Swiss educational system could be improved, he felt, all the negative aspects of the French Revolution could be avoided. It was not the destruction of the social structure that was needed, but the restoration of feelings of mutual respect and responsibility between the classes.

Under the new government Pestalozzi's patriotism was for a brief period provided with an outlet through the editorship of a paper, *The Helvetic People's Paper*. Its aim was to improve the general education of the populace, but it did not prove very successful. The content was too intellectual, and, with a large section of the population illiterate, it could have no widespread impact on precisely those people for whom it was primarily intended. After a few months as editor Pestalozzi, through a tragic event, was given a second and much more suitable post by the government. In September 1798 a French army, passing through the canton of Nidwald to attack the Austrians, met with armed opposition from a stubborn group of Swiss patriots who were not prepared to accept the presence of foreigners on their soil. So fiercely did the Swiss resist, that the French were violent and destructive in their retribution. They almost destroyed the town of Stans and thereby rendered many children homeless, some orphaned. The federal government, shocked by the viciousness of the attack, decided to set up a home for the children. An enthusiastic Pestalozzi was put in charge.

For nearly twenty years Pestalozzi's educational ideas had found no practical expression; over that period they had been fermenting, or perhaps stagnating. Now the supreme test had come for him, the 'death or success of my aims'.[1] Not only was this his last opportunity to convince the world at large that his ideas were not the fantasies of an eccentric, but also, at the age of fifty-two, he had to prove to himself that he had not wasted away his life in the pursuit of impracticable aims.

Pestalozzi had left his wife staying with a friend, and was therefore alone when in the December of 1798 he moved into the convent in Stans which had been assigned to him. The building itself was not complete, was unfurnished, and was still occupied by bricklayers and carpenters. There were other difficulties too. The first and foremost of these was the whole background of political turmoil against which the enterprise was to be carried out; a sense of stability, so essential to the upbringing of children, could not exist. Secondly, Pestalozzi had to face the continual hostility of the local population; this arose both because he was a Protestant in a Catholic district and because he was regarded as the emissary of the highly unpopular central government.

Pestalozzi's position was, therefore, not an enviable one. The needs of the children allowed for no postponement until the completion of the building or until a more satisfactory political situation developed. And so, immediately after Pestalozzi's own arrival, the children began to move in. Soon there were as many as eighty, of different ages, some from good family backgrounds, some but beggar children; many were dirty and some were ill. With these children Pestalozzi lived in the closest contact:

> From morning to evening I was virtually alone in their midst. Everything which benefited their bodies and souls came from my hand. Every piece of help, every form of succour in need which they received came directly from me. My hand lay in theirs; my eyes rested on theirs. My tears flowed with theirs and my smile accompanied theirs. They were outside the world, outside Stans, they were with me and I with them. Their soup was my soup, their drink, my drink. I had nothing, no servants, no friends, no helpers with me, I had only them. If they were healthy, I stood in their midst, if they were ill I was at their side. In the evening I was the last to go to bed, in the morning I was the first to get up.[2]

Surrounded by destitute and sometimes violent children Pestalozzi set out to win their confidence. Further difficulties arose even after the opening of the home. The children often fell ill as a result of the cold and damp of the convent. The problem was then aggravated by parents who blamed Pestalozzi for the illness and often enticed their children back home. Other parents waited until their children had been fed and clothed and then took them away. 'Months went by', wrote Pestalozzi, 'before I had the joy of being shaken by the hand by a father or a mother who gave me a cheerful, happy look.'[3] While some of the children remained refractory, the majority gradually became co-operative and enthusiastic:

> They felt that through me they were getting further than other children; they realized the inward connection between my guidance and their future life.[4]

Thus despite all the external obstacles Pestalozzi could write early in 1799:

> It is succeeding, it is succeeding in every way. I am blotting out the disgrace of my life. . . . I see and feel that my destiny is equal to that of other men, I myself have become a human being again and reconcile myself so gladly with my race.[5]

Pestalozzi had achieved his success by subordinating everything to establishing a relationship of love between himself and the children. By making love the foundation of the community at Stans, he found that the number and age of the pupils did not matter; indeed, to his joy he discovered that the more intelligent pupils were eager to pass on their knowledge to the less intelligent, who, in turn were eager to accept it. By his devotion to the children, he stimulated in them a desire to learn. He had realized that the actual process of learning was more than a means to an end: it was something of value, interest, and enjoyment in itself. Thus, when in June 1799 the convent was taken over as a military hospital and the experiment came to an abrupt end, Pestalozzi was not too disappointed. He had convinced himself that, by adopting his approach, education could be completely freed from the rigidity and inhumanity which prevailed at the time. It still remained for him to convince others.

5 · Burgdorf

After only a few weeks recovering from the strain of his work in Stans, Pestalozzi was given permission to teach in a school in the small town of Burgdorf. The town, built on a hill to the north of Bern, is dominated by its castle and it was in the castle itself that Pestalozzi had been allocated accommodation. The school was one of the two boys' schools in the town and was attended by the sons of those who were not full Burgdorf citizens. In charge of it was a cobbler named Dysli, with whom Pestalozzi was now going to share the teaching.

Teaching in Switzerland in the eighteenth century was not so much a professional activity as a menial task. Consequently there were few proper full-time teachers, the work of the teacher being carried out as a side-line by people who earned their living in some other way or by retired army officers or by anyone who needed to supplement his income with the teacher's meagre salary. It was often an occupation to which those were attracted who were capable of no other. Teachers were often unable to spell properly or to do the simplest arithmetic. Fortunately, such teachers were not expected to achieve much beyond teaching the children the catechism and supervising the class while pupils got on with individual work. Normally the only reading book used in class was the Bible. Anything which fell outside the daily routine of Bible-reading and the rote-learning of the catechism was liable to be regarded with suspicion.

It is therefore no small wonder that when Dysli's class of some seventy pupils was divided into two groups and the classroom into two halves by means of a chalk line, the contrast between the traditional teaching of the cobbler and the much more positive approach of Pestalozzi, with its emphasis on the importance of the teacher–pupil relationship, must have become unpleasantly blatant. The success of one person all too often breeds jealousy in another, and so it was with Dysli whose suspicion of the outsider quickly turned to dislike. Presumably fearing that Pestalozzi's aim was to dispossess him of his job, he began to spread rumours not only that the catechism was threatened but also that Pestalozzi could neither write nor do simple calculations and was not even capable of reading properly. Pestalozzi admits there was an element of truth in these accusations, but claims that he was able to turn the deficiencies in his own education to good advantage:

> I was able to teach writing without being able to write correctly myself, and my incapacity to do all these things was certainly very necessary in enabling me to attain both the greatest simplicity in teaching method and the means whereby the most untrained and unknowledgeable person could achieve success with his children.[1]

The cobbler persuaded the parents that the new schoolmaster was not beneficial to their children and he finally succeeded in dislodging his rival. Pestalozzi moved first to a small girls' school in the upper part of the town, and then, after an inspection of his work by the local school board, he was promoted to the more important of the two boys' schools. In the meantime J. R. Fischer, a young government official, had come to live in the castle where it was intended by the federal government that he should set up a national teachers' training college. Soon afterwards another young man, Hermann Krüsi, arrived to assist in the training, bringing with him a group of evacuee children from Appenzell, a part of Switzerland which had suffered particularly from the war. Fischer, after supervising Krüsi for a while, returned to Bern to try and solve some of the administrative difficulties which he was encountering in his attempts to establish the teachers' training college. But within a few weeks of leaving Burgdorf he died of typhoid fever. Pestalozzi was torn between feelings of sadness and joy – sadness at the loss of a close friend and joy because the possibility of his taking over the castle for an institute of his own now presented itself. His application to the government was granted and in October 1800 his new institute was opened. The first pupils included both fee-paying pupils from the town and the children from Appenzell whom Krüsi had brought. Krüsi himself became Pestalozzi's first assistant.

Pestalozzi had felt himself restricted while working in the schools of others, where the children did not seem to have reacted to his teaching as favourably as in Stans. But now, on his own, success came rapidly. At the beginning of the following year he wrote about his pupils to a friend:

> Imagine how it stirs my heart when alongside their great intellectual progress I see love, profound goodwill, and interest developing with equal rapidity in children who a few weeks before had been complete strangers. Imagine how it stirs my heart when even parents, with tears in their eyes, declare: I can see that my child is better; is more good-natured and kinder than before.[2]

Soon the importance of Pestalozzi's educational ideas and teaching methods was to be acknowledged not only by parents of children at the institute, but also by Europe at large. For Pestalozzi now requested a public inspection. As a result a two-man commission led by J. S. Ith, president of the Bernese Educational Council, visited the establishment in 1802. The two commissioners were most impressed by what they saw, and when they produced their report it helped to spread the reputation of Pestalozzi beyond the frontiers of Switzerland.

Increasing fame began to change the whole pattern of Pestalozzi's life. One of the changes which he most welcomed was the arrival of assistants to help him to teach the children and visitors to see his ideas put into practice. The assistants came from all walks of life. Krüsi himself had begun work as a day-labourer in his home-village and had then been persuaded to become the village schoolmaster. Some seven years later at the age of twenty-five he found himself as Pestalozzi's first assistant. Krüsi wrote enthusiastically of his new position to a friend who was studying theology at Basel and thereby gained another assistant for the new institute, Johann Tobler. In turn Tobler recommended Christoph Buss who had previously been a book-binder in Tübingen; when contacted he came to Burgdorf without even inquiring about his salary or conditions of employment. Also among the first arrivals was a young man who was to play an important part in Pestalozzi's life; his name was Johannes Niederer and he gave up his work as a village pastor in 1803 in order to join the institute. All these men with their different backgrounds were united by their idealism and their pioneering spirit. Pestalozzi was delighted at their arrival, for he was now in his mid-fifties and had long felt the need to pass on his ideas to others. In 1804 he wrote to Niederer:

> As long as you live our cause is not deserted. My conviction that you and Krüsi have been sent to me as saviours cannot be stronger. Daily I surrender myself up more and more to your strength. Your joining me makes me into something which I am not really and which, at my age, I never can become.[3]

As the years passed Pestalozzi was to become increasingly dependent on his assistants until, in the end, it was they who disposed of the ultimate fate of his educational enterprises.

The continual stream of visitors who now came to look at the institute at Burgdorf also gave Pestalozzi great satisfaction:

> Foreigners arrive daily from all parts to see, to examine, and even to participate, and I now contemplate the approaching end of my career with calm, as honest and careful attention is being almost universally paid to the essence of my activity.[4]

While his assistants developed his ideas and their practical applications, the visitors would proclaim the success of the new methods far and wide, thereby gaining for Pestalozzi new pupils and financial support.

Pestalozzi had always had detractors and as his reputation grew, the more vigorous did their attacks become. In the autumn of 1803 he found himself forced to write to the governments of the cantons of Appenzell and Glarus that 'Pastor Steinmüller of Gais has dared openly to publicize a completely false and groundless description of my method and my institute on the basis of a visit of three-quarters of an hour'.[5] With characteristic good-nature Pestalozzi suggested that Steinmüller should come to stay at the institute for a month and then give his judgement. Whereas his teaching methods could be defended against such open attacks, Pestalozzi considered that worse damage was done to his cause by those who, while supporting his methods, had really only a false conception of their basic principles. Rumour and misrepresentation were more dangerous than explicit criticism.

The growth of Pestalozzi's enterprise brought organizational changes also. The most positive of these was that Pestalozzi could now devote time to writing, and thereby to modifying his ideas in the light of practical experience. It was from 1800 onwards that he began to talk and write about his 'method'. The 'method' was not some clever new-found formula in any way contradicting his previous educational theories, but was a comprehensive concept for the basic principles which Pestalozzi suddenly felt must underlie all his separate theories and observations. In 1801 his most famous educational work, *How Gertrude teaches her Children*, appeared and in it he explains how his educational ideas had developed and how he had become increasingly aware that it should be possible to fit the ideas into one single system:

> For months I had worked at the elementary stages of instruction and done everything to reduce them to the greatest simplicity; yet I did not know how they fitted together, or at least I was not clearly conscious of how they did; with every hour, however, I felt that I was moving forwards, that I was moving quickly forwards.[6]

Never producing a definitive work expounding his 'method', Pestalozzi spent the rest of his life explaining how learning processes should be reduced to the simplest patterns and trying to show that these patterns did not conflict with each other but formed one harmonious whole.

However, not all the changes in Pestalozzi's life resulting from the establishment of his institute were beneficial. Indeed, Pestalozzi came to regard the period spent at Burgdorf as a turning-point in his life, a turning-point for the worse. He explains the reason in his *Swansong*, a work in which, at the age of eighty, he looked back over his past life:

> With the first step my foot made on the staircase in Burgdorf castle I was lost to myself in that I had entered on a career in which I could not be other than unhappy, for by accepting this post . . . I put myself in a position which presupposed as essential and necessary the capacity to wield authority which I lacked.[7]

In Burgdorf Pestalozzi ceased to be solely an educator and became the head of an organization. Unfortunately, to fulfil the latter function he had neither the self-assurance nor the business-sense.

How the deficiencies in Pestalozzi's character could put his whole enterprise in jeopardy were soon to be made all too clear. Between

1800 and 1803 the institute in the castle flourished. It was soon attended by over seventy pupils who were taught by about twenty assistants, some temporary. And then, when all seemed to be going well, political events intervened once again. At the end of 1802 Napoleon stated his determination to revise the Swiss constitution and Pestalozzi was one of the Swiss representatives who went to Paris for the consultations on the new constitution. However, Napoleon had already made up his mind on the form this would take and no formal discussions took place. Early in 1803 the Act of Mediation was signed by the Emperor, thereby dissolving the central government and restoring all administrative power to the cantons.

Pestalozzi had always enjoyed the support and encouragement of the central government, and it was thanks to its protection that he had obtained permission to teach in Burgdorf as well as to set up his own institute in the castle. The Bernese authorities, under whose jurisdiction the castle now fell, did not prove so co-operative. Almost immediately they informed Pestalozzi that the castle would have to be vacated by the summer of 1804 as it was required for a high government official. Attempts to revert the decision failed, but eventually alternative accommodation was offered in an empty convent at Münchenbuchsee, a small village not far from Bern. Only a mile away from the newly acquired building lay Hofwil where Daniel von Fellenberg, another pioneer in the educational field, kept his institute and his experimental farm. It was at this point that Pestalozzi made an unfortunate, if understandable, mistake. He agreed to combine his institute with that of Fellenberg. The plan seemed ideal because it would enable Pestalozzi to remain in charge of the educational side of his work, while the businesslike Fellenberg managed the financial and administrative side. But instead of the two men working in harmony, they came into conflict. In a letter to Fellenberg written after the partnership had already broken up Pestalozzi outlined their differing attitudes:

> I saw your strength but also knew of what I, with my weaknesses, was capable. I esteemed your sense of order but knew also the value of the unconstrained atmosphere which had been the hallmark of my institute until then. I valued your internal and external methods of administration, but at the same time I knew that without

> any of these methods the hearts of my household were drawn to me. I recognized the advantage of allocating responsibility, but knew of the effects of love which can surpass anything that mere responsibility can do. . . .[8]

Later in life Pestalozzi was to admit that many of his setbacks had been his own fault, for he had tried to supplement deficiencies in his own character by making use of the complementary capacities in others.

Fortunately, the consequences of the disagreement were not as disastrous as they might have been, for when Pestalozzi had been forced to leave Burgdorf, he had been offered the castle at Yverdon in the Canton of Vaud as well as the building in Münchenbuchsee and wisely he had decided to accept them both. Whereas pupils and staff were divided between the two places, Pestalozzi himself spent more and more time at Yverdon as relations with Fellenberg became increasingly strained. When in the Autumn of 1804 the final parting of the ways came, the assistants who had gone to Münchenbuchsee rejoined Pestalozzi at Yverdon. Yet even here the happy atmosphere of the Burgdorf days could not be restored – the enterprise had grown too large, the assistants too numerous for a man who, in the words of his assistant Krüsi, was capable of 'stimulating, teaching, and inspiring, but not of organizing'.[9]

6 · The Rise and Fall of the Yverdon Institute

How radically the course of Pestalozzi's life had altered since the days at Stans when for several months he had alone looked after the education of a large group of children! It had been a time when he had lived 'as if in a fairy world' and 'in the full realization of my dreams'.[1] Whereas the success he had enjoyed there had been personal and intimate, the success which came to him at Yverdon was the very opposite. Here the eye of publicity scrutinized his every movement, assessed and criticized his every achievement. In Stans success or failure in his enterprises rested alone with him, but here there were others who were ready to appropriate praise to themselves while putting the blame on colleagues. As in Burgdorf, Pestalozzi remained a source of inspiration, a subject for admiration, and yet he was no longer the master of his fate:

> I am in my enterprise like a boat lost in the raging seas. The control of my enterprise rests no more in my hands; I am in its power and must let myself be swept along wherever it wishes. So far its course has been smooth and strong, yet I follow it with a trembling heart – it is beyond my strength to resist.[2]

Pestalozzi sensed approaching disaster but was powerless to prevent it.

Initially there were seventy pupils at Yverdon, but by 1809 this figure had more than doubled and prospective pupils had to be turned down. Most of the children were fee-paying, but Pestalozzi always managed to arrange for some poor children to attend free. The age of entry varied; Pestalozzi considered that six was the best age to enter, but was prepared to accept pupils up to the age of about twelve. With the number of pupils, the number of teachers also increased, and often outnumbering these were the teachers in training who were sometimes sent by educational authorities and sometimes came on their own initiative. The most important group were those sent by the Prussian Ministry of Education during and after 1809. They spent three years in the institute, and this greatly pleased Pestalozzi for he always felt his method was threatened by those who only acquired a half-knowledge of it. The very size of his enterprise, as well as his old age – he was now over sixty – demanded that he should delegate responsibility to some of his assistants. The two on whose shoulders the task mainly fell were Niederer and Johannes Schmid. Niederer, who had had a philosophical training, became the spokesman of Pestalozzi, expounding his theories and defending him from adverse criticism. So immersed and self-assured did Niederer become in this work that Pestalozzi ironically made the remark that anyone seeking his opinion on any subject would be advised to turn to Niederer, who could expound it so much better than he could himself. Schmid was a hard, practical man, whose abilities were devoted to the administration of the institute; as a former pupil of the institute at Burgdorf, he had a special place in Pestalozzi's heart. Both assistants played an essential role in setting the tone in the institute which could only be expected to flourish as long as they remained in harmony with each other and with the rest of the staff. Once the pioneering spirit, the idealism, and the mutual respect which bound Pestalozzi to his assistants and his assistants to each other, faded, then the continued existence of the institute would be set in jeopardy.

A daily routine soon established itself in the castle. The children got up at half past five, the first lesson beginning at six. Morning prayers followed at seven and afterwards the children washed, tidied themselves up, and ate breakfast. Lessons kept them busy between eight and midday. There followed lunch which was the main meal of the day and consisted of soup, meat and vegetables, bread, and a glass of wine. After lunch the children were free until half past one when lessons restarted and continued until half past three. Then, until five, there was another break during which the children were given some bread and fruit. More lessons followed until eight. In the remaining hour before bed-time the children ate their supper and attended prayers. On Sunday mornings the children attended church in the town, in the afternoons went on a long walk, and in the evenings attended an assembly during which Pestalozzi mentioned points of discipline and behaviour and any other matters which had arisen during the week; on rare occasions he tactfully, but effectively, admonished individual pupils who had misbehaved.

Three times a week after the evening meal there were meetings of the teachers. One of these was devoted to discussing the children, another to the more practical problems which the teachers had encountered during the week, and the third to the 'method'. The principles of the 'method' were being applied to various subjects by the assistants. Of all, Schmid was proving the most successful. Pestalozzi was so pleased with his attempts to modernize the techniques of mathematics teaching that in 1807 he wrote of him: 'If God gives him but two years of similar progress, education, as far as mathematics is concerned, will have been altered for ever and ever.'[3] Schmid's success not only increased his own self-assurance, but naturally raised him even more highly in Pestalozzi's estimation. Greater prestige inevitably brought Schmid into conflict with Niederer, and finally a crisis developed in their relationship which not only led to the departure of Schmid from the institute in 1810, but also to his publication of a work attacking Niederer which brought the whole institute into disrepute.

Schmid's departure was not the only indication of impending difficulties. In 1809 Pestalozzi had requested another official inspection of his institute in the hope that the method might yet be considered suitable to form the basis for a national system of education. The request had been granted and a six-day inspection led by Father Girard of Fribourg had ensued. When, however, the report finally appeared in 1810, it was not filled with the unqualified praise for which Pestalozzi had hoped. On the contrary, by examining each aspect of the institute's work in detail, the commission had found much to criticize, and while acknowledging its successes, especially in the field of moral education, it concluded that it could not be set up as an example for the whole of Switzerland to admire and emulate.

With Girard's report and Schmid's departure the institute set into a gradual decline. Some of the most faithful teachers left to take up other posts, and in 1813 the Prussian teachers departed to fight for their country against Napoleon. In 1814 there was even a threat that the castle would be taken over as a military hospital. The municipal authorities of Yverdon, fearing disease would be brought into the town, sent two emissaries to the headquarters of the allied forces in Basel in order to try and revoke the decision. Pestalozzi, uninvited, attached himself to the two men who reluctantly accepted his company. On their return, however, they were the first to acknowledge that it was due to Pestalozzi that their mission had succeeded. Pestalozzi had been granted an audience by the Tsar, and had talked to him enthusiastically about popular education. Even if the Tsar's interest was theoretical rather than practical, at least he saved the castle from occupation. Pestalozzi never lost an opportunity of establishing contact with people of power and influence who might further his method in the territories in which they governed. When, for instance, he heard that the King of Prussia was in the nearby town of Neuchatel, he insisted on getting up from the bed where he had been lying ill in order to thank the monarch for the interest he had shown in elementary education. Unfortunately, Pestalozzi's attempts to convert the great never really met with success.

Since 1810 the financial difficulties of the institute had also increased. Niederer fully recognized his incapacity to deal with the worsening situation and persuaded Pestalozzi to write to Schmid and ask him to return. Schmid agreed and took up his post again in 1815. If, on his return, Schmid had concerned himself solely with righting the institute's finances, Pestalozzi's enterprise might well have regained its former influence and renown. However he was not content to play a subsidiary part in the running of the institute. Instead, he applied himself to an organization of every aspect of the life at Yverdon. The happy freedom enjoyed by the staff was replaced by the strictest discipline. The castle became a police state where, in Krüsi's words, 'the lower civil servants had, as unquestioning agents, to carry out the orders of higher officials'.[4] The moment of crisis had arrived; in the Spring of 1816 a large number of teachers resolved to put up with the situation no longer and resigned. Among them was Krüsi, Pestalozzi's first assistant, who had remained with him through the fifteen years during which he had achieved European fame. Niederer remained for a few months and then he too made the break with Pestalozzi. With all his closest assistants gone, Pestalozzi, now over seventy years of age, became all the more dependent on Schmid. The institute dragged on an existence for a further eight years until in 1825 Schmid's enemies found some pretext for having an official order issued for his expulsion from the Canton of Vaud. Pestalozzi, now nearly eighty years old, threw in his lot with that of his assistant and left with him. The last two years of Pestalozzi's life were spent in the Neuhof, where half a century before he had begun his task of transforming educational concepts and attitudes. Even here, however, he was not left in peace by his critics. Many years previously in 1808 he had written:

> I almost think that now would be the time to die so that I do not lose again that which I now possess. I cannot be happier than I am at present; but it may well be that after so much happiness I could not bear sorrow as well as I have done until now.[5]

This inward wish had not come true, and unfortunately in the disintegration of the administrative side of his life's work, his vision and his theories had lost some of their impetus. It was under these sad circumstances, almost directly after receiving a further defamatory pamphlet attacking him and his work, that he died in February, 1827.

The decline of the Yverdon institute can be attributed in the main to its organizer's incapacity to prevent his assistants from coming into conflict with each other. There was also his failure to maintain financial security. If the causes of the ultimate failure at Yverdon are apparent, so are the reasons of Pestalozzi's success in establishing and developing the Burgdorf and Yverdon institutes. It was in part the very lack of rigid organization, the free and unrestricted discipline, which attracted assistants to Pestalozzi. Their devotion to him became clear enough when some of them were expected to fulfil their function in Fellenberg's clockwork organization. Pestalozzi's attitude was radically different from that of Fellenberg:

> My opinion is that such a society can only succeed if each member of it is free to go astray and to make mistakes, and is able rather through quiet experience than correction to realize himself and to make as much progress as his own character allows of.[6]

Yet in the same letter written in 1806 Pestalozzi indicated that such freedom of action was not easy to maintain:

> There are moments when the heroes of our community want to call down fire from heaven because all are not pulling on the common rope as they would wish it. In such cases I always pour water upon the fire.[7]

But, naturally, as Pestalozzi grew older he became less able to moderate authoritatively between opposing factions, and as his assistants began to feel more and more indispensable they took up increasingly intransigent positions. Yet for many years, by the sheer force of his personality, Pestalozzi had been able not only to hold his enterprise together, but to drive it forward. Physically he was the very opposite of a compelling figure. A former pupil described him as:

> a very ugly man with bristly hair, a face lined with smallpox scars and covered with freckles, an irregular and prickly beard, with no neckerchief; a man whose badly buttoned trousers drooped over his socks as these did over his rough shoes; a man with a panting, jerky walk, with eyes which at one moment sparkled, wide open, and at another closed in inward contemplation, with features which sometimes reflected a deep sorrow and then sometimes the purest joy, with a voice which was now hesitating and now impetuous, now soft and harmonious, and now storming like thunder.[8]

Despite his outward appearance and manner, Pestalozzi long succeeded in holding pupils and masters alike in bonds of affection and admiration. The same former pupil wrote:

> We all loved him, as he loved us all; we loved him so deeply that we were sad when we did not see him for a time, and when he returned we could not turn our eyes away from him.[9]

Niederer tried to analyse more specifically what it was that inspired those with whom he came into contact:

> His age, the realization of what he had achieved, his fatherly attitude, his completely incomparable and inimitable originality in appearance, word, and action, his engaging effect on the heart, and his magic and electric effect on the intellect and on the imagina-

> tion stimulated the highest in them – a conception and consciousness of the invisible and the ideals this inspired.[10]

Perhaps, for more than any other reason, he was able to attract others to his cause, because he had so totally accepted it himself.

Pestalozzi, in the practical side of his work, owed much to the help and support of others; however, the originality of his educational ideas and the urgency with which he felt they should be put into practice separated him off from his fellow-countrymen:

> Throughout my life I have sought the basic elements of the faculties and capacities which my country needs more urgently now than ever before. Often I went astray, often I made mistakes, but often I seemed to have gone astray, I seemed to have made mistakes just because I was *alone*, and here and there there have been those who more than smiled when, quietly sitting on their chairs in their rooms sipping their tea and smoking their pipes, they saw the poor toiler running about looking for a good and advantageous path over mountain and valley, and saw him neglecting and destroying himself in bog and thicket for his cause. I was seeking the path for their children and for a country which was their country and my country.[11]

If Pestalozzi could have known that the principles of education which he had expounded would be universally acknowledged, he would gladly have accepted all the failures and misfortunes of the final years of his life. His own assessment of his life would rest, as ours must too, on whether these principles are as universal and as valid as he himself believed.

PART TWO

Pestalozzi's Educational Ideas

7 · Introduction to Pestalozzi's 'Method'

What was it in the teaching methods of his time against which Pestalozzi reacted so violently? A description of a school period by a contemporary of his should give a clear indication:

> Every day the first period was devoted to reading the Bible. We began at the place where we had left off the day before until we had 'finished' the Bible. Then we immediately restarted at the first word of the first book of Genesis and continued through to the last word of the Revelation of John. Thus we went through the Old Testament, the Apocrypha, and the New Testament; not a single word was left out. We really achieved something, for in about eight months we had got through. That is good going. It can be explained, however, when one realizes that absolutely nothing was clarified, and that it was the 'done thing' to read away as quickly as possible without any expression or a single hesitation. For this reason we always looked forward to the Books of Chronicles, in which there were so many difficult names one after the other and one did not have to think. In fact in other places too one very rarely did because everything rushed past far too quickly. The pupils read in turn and during the period the Headmaster seldom said more than the word: 'Next!' when another pupil had to continue. At the most he corrected a word which had been pronounced wrongly or called to someone who had not been following, 'Next!' even though it was not his turn. If he stumbled, he was struck a few times with the cane. For us the Bible was no more than a reader which was only of interest to us because with its help we could show how well and quickly we were able to read. The contents were mostly incomprehensible to us, especially to the

D

> children who spoke dialect; moreover we did not pay much attention to the contents. Of course, we knew the Bible was God's word; but we did not really understand what that meant. For us the title-page, the prefaces, and the chapter headings were equally God's word because they were in the Bible, and if the bookbinder had felt like binding another book in with the Bible we would not have doubted but that it was equally God's word.[1]

The cruelty of the schoolmasters, the severity of the discipline have possibly been exaggerated as causes of Pestalozzi's attitude. Certainly he was completely opposed to all forms of inhumanity in the classroom, yet by no means all teachers would have depended on rule by force of the cane. Pestalozzi's criticism was far more basic and universal than the maltreatment of pupils in certain schools, for he accused the whole system – both the methods and the content – of having become fettered by routine and tradition, to the point where teaching had degenerated into cramming and where school subjects had become no more than a particular selection of facts to be learnt by heart. Teaching methods had become so rigid that they took into account neither the capacities of a child to learn what was placed in front of him, nor the purpose for which he was expected to do so.

> The most important mistake of present-day education is undoubtedly the following: Too much is expected of the child and too many of the topics only appear to be something but are nothing.[2]

Schools instead of acting with nature, and stimulating and encouraging the child, seemed to do everything to stunt originality and the imagination. For children entry to school after some five years of freedom was a form of punishment:

> Suddenly the whole of nature around them is made to vanish from their sight, the attractive expression of their spontaneity and their freedom is tyrannically stopped; shoved into groups they are thrown like sheep into a stinking room, they are chained mercilessly for hours, days, weeks, months, and years, and forced to look at miserable, unattractive and monotonous letters and to follow a whole way of life capable of driving them mad, so different is it from their previous existence.[3]

Schools had become no more than 'artificial machines to stifle all the achievements of strength and experience which nature herself brings to life within them'.[4]

To replace old methods Pestalozzi wanted to introduce a new system of education which would take fully into account the child himself, what he was capable of achieving mentally and physically, and what he was capable of experiencing spiritually. While bearing in mind a child's future station in adult life, education was to become 'child-centred' and adapt itself to the intelligence, feelings, and enthusiasms of the children. This system, which he hoped would be established universally, Pestalozzi called his 'method'. The 'method' was far more than a system of recommended class-room procedures:

> People are completely mistaken in assuming without good reason that my aims are limited to facilitating the elementary skills of reading, writing, and arithmetic. They are not! My purpose does not stop here but probes deeply into the very essence of higher intellectual and moral education and into the most thorough investigations of human nature itself.[5]

The 'method' was a philosophical concept, an ultimate value, which can perhaps best be defined as 'the ideal method of developing a child's personality and capacities to the full and of preparing him to live a full and happy life as an adult'. Of course, such a definition is not very revealing, but it does emphasize two features of Pestalozzi's 'method'. It recognizes an ideal which every effort should be made to approach; the existing passive acceptance of old forms should be replaced by active interest in the educational field. The structure of society was changing and education could and should play an important part in these changes. The second feature which needs to be stressed is the empirical approach to education allowed by a system where there are no definite boundaries. The test of any educational theory lay in its practical application, and therefore Pestalozzi did not concern himself whether any idea was new or original nor whether it could logically be fitted into existing theories, as long as it proved to be beneficial to the child.

A reputation can be a dangerous thing to have, and that of Pestalozzi's 'method' was such that people came to imagine that it was some entirely new magic formula. Yet on examination many of the theories seemed to have been advocated before, and the men who were attempting to put them into practice seemed anything but magicians. And so, not finding what they had expected, critics blamed Pestalozzi for their own misconceptions, pointing out that many of his ideas were not original, and deeming this a fault. In fact, Pestalozzi had never claimed that his theories were entirely new, nor did he regard originality for its own sake as a virtue:

> It is in no way my intention to stress any one of my points of view because it is new; I hold fast to my system because I believe it consistent with human nature, and I am convinced that educational theory in all aspects in which it is fully developed, corresponds to that which is true in my system. I am convinced that every good educationist was more or less on the scent of my most important ideas. Indeed I believe even the Greeks employed methods of teaching which in spirit and in form were similar to mine. It is absolutely certain that every good father and every good mother will be naturally forced within the family circle to make use of the whole range of my method's elementary principles.[6]

Even if Pestalozzi's ideas considered singly were not all original, and despite efforts of critics to play them down, the impact of the ideas is undeniable. For Pestalozzi not only had positive ideas but also had the personality and perseverance to force them on the attention of an age which hovered between revolution and conservatism, an age which needed yet feared change.

> 'It is fairly generally felt in towns and villages alike that schools are not what they should be.'
>
> 'Indeed! But when it is a matter of changing them, everyone cries out: "The old system is good!" and clings to it for grim death.'[7]

8 · The General Principles of Pestalozzi's 'Method'

Pestalozzi never produced a comprehensive description of all his educational theories. Despite this, certain ideas recur again and again in his works. It is therefore possible to talk of the general principles which Pestalozzi made into a foundation for his educational theories and practice. In *How Gertrude teaches her Children* Pestalozzi explains how he was exposing his views to a friend without being able to sum up his main aim in any simple catch-phrase when the friend suddenly exclaimed: 'You want to mechanize education.'[1] Pestalozzi found the description apt, but, like all over-simplified definitions, it must be interpreted correctly. If the friend had said to Pestalozzi: 'You want to humanize education', his definition would have been equally valid. An outline of Pestalozzi's general principles should help to show that the apparently contradictory definitions are useful and can be reconciled.

Pestalozzi was the first to acknowledge the heritage he had received from Rousseau – the man who had been 'the turning point between the old and new worlds of education'.[2] It was Rousseau who had condemned contemporary educational methods as 'unnatural':

> Powerfully gripped by all-powerful nature, realizing as no other the separation of his fellow-men from the strong influence of the senses and from intellectual life, he broke with Herculean strength the chains of the mind, and gave the child back to himself and education back to the child and to human nature.[3]

Pestalozzi took over the concept that education must harmonize with nature. However simple such a plan might seem when one bears in mind the rigid, stultified system of the time, Pestalozzi and his followers regarded it as outspoken and revolutionary. Their attitude emerges clearly in the following description by Niederer of the method's aim:

> The principle of Pestalozzi when he took over the castle and founded the Institute (i.e. at Burgdorf) was revolutionary. By word and deed he wanted to tear down and build up again: tear down the whole school system as it had existed up to then, a system which appeared to him monstrous; then to build up a new school system in which he wanted to entrust the subjects taught to the basic elements and methods of nature. The subjects taught had to be adapted to the nature of the child, to the range of activity of which he was capable, to the stage of his development and to his individual needs. The basic elements of instruction he wished to educe from the physical, mental, moral, and religious nature of the child, from its elemental appearances. The course of instruction had to be brought into complete harmony with the stages of development of human nature.[4]

The passage already gives an impression of the methods Pestalozzi considered necessary in order to render education more 'natural'. The early part of the passage underlines the vigour with which Pestalozzi felt they would have to be propagated if they were to replace the old methods.

It is not surprising to find that Pestalozzi uses a natural image to convey one of his most fundamental principles:

> Man, imitate the action of great nature which from the seed of even the largest tree pushes at first but an imperceptible shoot, but then by a further imperceptible growth which progresses smoothly every hour and every day unfolds the young trunk, then that which will grow into the main branches, then the subsidiary branches, and finally the smallest twigs from which will hang the ephemeral leaves. Notice how nature tends and protects each single part formed and how she attaches each new part to the strong life of the old.[5]

Pestalozzi did not see the new-born child as a rough-hewn stone into which parents and educators could carve the image they wanted, but as a seed which already contained the essence of the child's intelligence and personality. The aim of his method was to provide the stimulation necessary to enable the elementary potential of the child to be developed to the full. Thus Pestalozzi's view of the influence of heredity on the one hand and environment on the other corresponds to the modern assessment of their relative roles. Heredity does have a vital influence on mental, personal, and physical characteristics – but this influence can be almost completely annulled if during the first years of life the child's environment represses his capacities.

The belief that talents were inborn and not imposed from outside did not in any way reduce the importance of parents and teachers. Indeed the art of education lay in providing the correct exercises and a satisfactory background for the child's talents to develop to the full. Pestalozzi's claim was that in presenting material in an educational form to the child, there was an ideal order in which to present it. To establish what this order was, it was necessary to reduce a topic to its most fundamental elements and then build it up gradually from there step by step. The development of a topic from the most simple to the most difficult should be divided up into as many gradations as possible. To do this did not involve discovering any new material but merely laying bare and interpreting facts which were already known. The method

> aims at finding and grasping essential elements, i.e. the unalterable points of departure and links of all instruction and all education. It aims at uncovering, not discovering, the elements.[6]

By grouping facts and experiences together in the right way, by arranging them in the right order, it should be possible to establish a natural progression from the most simple to the most difficult without there being any gaps. Pestalozzi gave a clear indication of how this progression was to be established:

> First of all learn to arrange your observations and to complete the elementary before proceeding to something complicated. In every aspect of education try to organize a progression of experiences in which each new concept is a small, almost unnoticeable addition to former experiences already firmly engrained and never to be forgotten by you.[7]

The progression from simple to difficult could not emerge merely from studying the relevant material; if it were to be used to teach children it must take child psychology into consideration. For Pestalozzi the art of the teacher lay in ensuring that the level of difficulty of the subject matter corresponded exactly to the child's developing capacity to comprehend. He insisted that instruction had to be based on a child's understanding, not on that of an adult. Hence education was for him child-centred, and to be successful depended on close observation of children and on deep insight into the way a child's mind works and develops. Pestalozzi therefore proposed empirical methods to educe the ways in which educational material should be presented to the children:

> That which he (the teacher) wishes to impart to his children, he must have mastered himself as thoroughly as he wishes them to master it. He can best achieve this if he often learns with and alongside the children, and thereby places himself in a position not only to gain a complete grasp of the subject with which he wishes to become acquainted, but also to observe the children themselves and all their reactions when learning; he should notice how he can stimulate and direct the awakening faculties of each child and how he brings them step by step closer to the goal which he has decided upon.[8]

If close observation was to be the means of discovering the ideal method of education, the interest shown by the child would be the best indication of the success of any method. For a child would only be interested by that which he could fully understand and that which was presented to him in an exciting form:

> His desire to develop his mental powers by exercising them will necessarily diminish if the means whereby it is hoped to teach him to think do not appeal in an attractive way to his mental faculties, but only irritate him by their tedium, and subdue and confuse him rather than stimulate and arouse him by their harmony.[9]

There is an interesting similarity between Pestalozzi's approach and that of the modern Swiss psychologist, Jean Piaget, who by extensive observation and experiment, has tried to show how a child's capacity to comprehend the world around him develops, pointing out that often a child's comprehension of certain phenomena and concepts follows a strict chronological order. It follows that a child cannot understand what one might call concept C until he has understood concepts A and B. Pestalozzi's view that all experience and information must be provided in a certain order which corresponds to a child's age and ability to understand is, therefore, upheld by modern opinion.

Because the method was based on developing the natural talents of the child, it had not only to take child psychology into account, but also had to examine the character and intelligence of the individual child:

> Inasmuch as the method is positive, it bases itself directly on the individual child which it has in its care; indeed there is nothing positive in education and in teaching but the individual child and the individual talents he has.[10]

Instead of presenting material to children and leaving it to chance what they retained, the teacher's function, according to Pestalozzi, was to find out the capacities of each individual child and thereby which stage in the natural progression from simple to difficult within each sphere of education he had reached. No longer would the child have to adapt himself as best he could to the material presented to him; instead he would be taught in a class where his individual needs would be catered for.

So far we have considered the analytical aspect of Pestalozzi's theories: his desire to reduce educational topics to their basic elements and then build them up again in a natural progression from simple to difficult in accordance with a child's growing capacity to comprehend. For this purpose Pestalozzi recognized three basic aspects of education: Intellectual education, moral education, and practical education (i.e. physical education in the broadest sense). A chapter will be devoted to each of the three aspects. Here, however, it should be noted that while Pestalozzi attempted to break the educational process down into basic elements in order to simplify and rationalize it, he insisted that it was the whole personality which had to be educated:

> Nature forms the child as an indivisible whole, as a vital organic unity with many-sided moral, mental, and physical capacities. She wishes that none of these capacities remain undeveloped. Where nature has influence and the child is well and truly guided by her, she develops the child's heart, mind, and body in harmonious unity.

> The development of the one is not only indivisibly linked with the development of the other, but each of these capacities is developed through and by means of the others.[11]

Again we find Pestalozzi upholding a modern view – for in the past it has often wrongly been maintained that abilities compensated for each other: for example, a good athlete would often prove a poor pupil in the class-room, a bright pupil would often prove bad at games. It has now been shown that there is a high correlation between the various human abilities, i.e. the bright pupil is likely to do quite well at games, the poor pupil is likely to be weak at them. In trying to educate the whole personality, Pestalozzi was interested in every aspect of education – hence the interest of so many of his contemporaries in his work.

The aim of Pestalozzi's method was not only to develop the individual to the full, but also to benefit every child whatever his age or class or future profession. By basing his system on the natural growth of a child's capacities, he could rightly claim that it was universally applicable. Through the method the various types of education – general and professional, private and public, working class and middle class – would be seen to have a common basis. Pestalozzi had no desire to make the system more uniform, but felt that every type of teaching could be related to every other type and that by so doing, the aim and limits of each type would become more clearly defined. He did not believe that each individual was capable of reaching the same standards of attainment, but he did insist that each and every child should have the chance to develop those talents which he had to the full. Of the treatment of pupils in Yverdon he wrote:

> In our dealings with the children we make no distinctions which are based on outward things or on matters of chance. In these respects we recognize absolutely no superiority in the merit of one child over another except to be and to become that which, according to the strength of his will and the degree of his effort and self-control, he can be and should become. We acknowledge humanity, i.e. human nature, in all alike.[12]

By emphasizing that which every child had in common, not that which separated them, Pestalozzi maintained that his method could help everyone in every stage of development.

From this summary of Pestalozzi's general principles, the humanizing and mechanizing elements in his theories should have become clear. By ordering knowledge and experiences, he hoped to find an ideal way in which to teach children, and methods which would prove universally applicable. At the same time by continually stressing that education was for the child and not the child for education, he showed that the needs of the individual child had to be taken into account. Education was to become at the same time more human and more scientific.

As we now turn to the three main aspects of education – the moral, intellectual, and practical – we shall try to mention not only the theoretical ideas of Pestalozzi, but also how the ideas worked out in practice. Pestalozzi neither had the time nor the knowledge to break down every educational topic into elements. He therefore depended much on his assistants. Some were inevitably more successful than others. Some topics were carefully examined, some only cursorily, and some were completely neglected. Pestalozzi warned his critical contemporaries against judging his method too hastily:

> By examining my aims closely, no decisive, certain judgement on them is possible; even an examination of how the method is being put into practice in the institute does not make a fundamental judgement possible. The extensive subdivisions of the method, the numerous personalities of the institute, make an overall assessment very difficult. Some of the peculiarities of both are too far removed from normal teaching and are linked too closely and deeply to the emergence and development of the whole for their real nature to be assessed by any general examination or survey. The matter may appear in terms of personalities, some of whom may not appear very appealing, some even directly repellant; he who seeks the truth must be able to overcome this impression and distinguish it clearly from the object under examination.[13]

There was the danger that both theories and practice would be misinterpreted. Pestalozzi, however, never claimed that his ideas had been perfected. From the assertion that there was an ideal method of presenting educational topics to pupils to the point where the method could be claimed to be effective, let alone perfect, much experimentation was necessary. In a single institute at a time, without national support, with a staff who were often not in complete harmony, the long task could only be begun. Therefore we must avoid condemning too categorically the illogical or the superseded in Pestalozzi's work, and remember that he would have been the first to condemn and reject any aspect of his educational practice which had been shown inadequate or capable of improvement.

9 · Intellectual Education

Pestalozzi was clear in his mind where lay the difference between his methods of instruction and those of his contemporaries:

> In the one case the child and all his capacities will be stimulated earlier and activated, in the other the innermost being of the child will be forced into an emptiness, a desert, which despite the skill with which the world attempts to conceal it, will appear obvious to everyone from the moment its opposite has been shown to be undeniably true.[1]

Whatever pupils were being taught, Pestalozzi insisted that it was wrong to impose knowledge on them from 'outside'. On the contrary it was necessary to stimulate them from within. Instruction did not consist of 'teaching pupils about thought, but of forming their capacity to think'.[2] Teachers, therefore, had to reject the conventional teaching methods and begin to analyse the mental processes of the child in order to discover how the concepts a child could comprehend depended on his age and his stage of development. By adopting such an approach, teachers would be teaching according to Pestalozzi's method:

> The method develops of itself out of the human mind. All who were put on the track of the method, all, even young children, found it within themselves. The talents and capacities of the youngest children developed along the same lines, according to the same laws, from the same starting point, as those of the teacher. The first teachers at the institute sought and followed the track of the method, just as the youngest children sought and followed it.[3]

The teacher was thus faced with the task of regrouping and adapting the knowledge which the child had to acquire in such a way that it would be immediately comprehensible, even obvious, to him. At the same time the teacher had to avoid imparting mere facts and ensure that the child had a real grasp of the essence of a particular subject.

The first aim was to find the simplest starting-point and then build up from there. Pestalozzi described his attempts to do this at Burgdorf:

> I tried in every way to make the elements of spelling and arithmetic as simple as possible and to put them in such a way that the child could be brought with great psychological skill from the first stage only gradually to the second – but then without any gaps in his knowledge remaining – and that then, basing himself on the fully comprehended second stage, he could be brought quickly and surely to the third and fourth stages.[4]

As an indication of how to adapt subjects to form a natural progression from simple to complex, Pestalozzi made the interesting suggestion that concepts might be presented to children in the same order as the human race had grasped them. Whether such a method is really valid for actually discovering the ideal order seems doubtful. In some subjects, especially scientific ones, the whole approach can change so radically from one generation to the next that it would be a retrograde step to show how the human race had accepted an inadequate approach before adopting a more modern one. Also it would be difficult to have enough historical information to follow correctly the acquisition of concepts by the human race. In all events Pestalozzi himself never made a study of history to try and find the order, but relied solely on a process of trial and error. The historical parallel does, however, help to give us an idea of what Pestalozzi was seeking.

If the teacher is not to impose ideas on the child from outside, then he must rely on the child and his immediate environment for the knowledge he wishes to impart. For this reason the child's environment and his capacity for perceiving this environment become of essential importance in Pestalozzi's theory of intellectual education. Before a child can ever draw conclusions about the world around him, he must have learnt to assess it properly:

> The withholding of judgement until we have seen and heard enough and only then . . . to talk and judge from the fullness of one's

conviction is truly the essential factor in bringing men to reflection and wisdom.[5]

Observation must precede judgement:

Nature only leads men gradually to thoughts and abstractions; in an infinite variety she places before us thousands of objects and pictures. To observe these pictures in the right way is the means to comprehend correctly the differences which exist between all things.[6]

The child had to learn to use his senses properly and fully before he could progress from 'observations to clear concepts'. A mother entrusted her three-year-old son to Pestalozzi for private tuition:

I tried through letters, pictures, everything which lay near to hand to teach him – in other words, by these means to produce in him – certain concepts and reflections. I made him specifically name everything he knew about each object – colour, parts, position, shape, and number. I was soon forced to put aside the first torment of youth, the miserable alphabet; he only wanted to look at pictures and objects which lay within the circle of his experience.[7]

Asking himself what his real contribution to education was, Pestalozzi answered that it lay in his establishing the first and foremost law of education: observation is the absolute basis of all knowledge.

So far we have considered how knowledge essential to a child should best be presented to him. It is, however, not possible to discuss the manner of instruction without considering its matter. Pestalozzi, when he stated that in Yverdon 'we consider the subjects in which we give instruction more as a means of training the mind than as a means of extending knowledge',[8] was emphasizing what he regarded as the aim of instruction. But he did not believe that the aim could be attained by divorcing matter from manner:

On the contrary, we are convinced that the true and general elements and principles for training the mind are at the same time the general, immutable elements and points of departure of the subjects themselves, and that there are no others nor can there be.[9]

Pestalozzi was not attacking the actual content of education, but the way in which it was presented – as dry facts rather than as living experience. School subjects had become too isolated and their educational, as opposed to their purely practical, function had become neglected. Therefore when Pestalozzi attempted to reduce education to its most simple elements, he rejected the division of knowledge into subjects and instead divided it into what he considered the three basic mental processes. All elementary education, he claimed, was based on language, number, and form – an interesting parallel to verbal ability, numerical ability, and spatial ability, which the intelligence tests of today try to assess. The child would have to use language, number, and form in order to understand and assess the information he received from his senses. Nor were they essential merely to the recognition of truth, but to its discovery also. In other words, language, number, and form did not only provide pigeon-holes into which knowledge could be placed, but set the mind in motion in the right way so that it would be able to recognize the knowledge in the first place. It followed that elementary education must make the child as familiar as possible with the three forms of mental process.

Language, for Pestalozzi, was more than a means of communication:

> Language . . . is indispensable to the development of our humanity. . . . To man language is given as a means of expressing his reflections, his feelings, his aims, his hopes, and his worries. Language is in itself . . . the essence of the mental consciousness the human race has of itself and of nature. Therefore as every *human* activity is inseparable from consciousness and only through the latter reveals itself according to its nature as human, so is talking inseparable from all human learning and activity. Just as the child cannot become clearly conscious of his natural observations and impressions without language, so will he not be able to attain knowledge of the very first element of number and form.[10]

Because of the link between language and consciousness, the mother-tongue held the most important place in Pestalozzi's teaching.

Analysing the various aspects of language teaching, Pestalozzi divided it up into (1) the teaching of sounds and words, (2) grammar and sentence structure, and (3) language as meaning. Before the child came to school, his mother should have encouraged his first attempts at speech and allowed him to experiment with sounds. She should also have taught him the names of all the everyday objects around him.

Only when the child was capable of distinguishing the various sounds by ear should the teaching of spelling and reading begin. Already in Stans, Pestalozzi had begun to develop an exercise which he found effective and in which:

> all the consonants are placed in front of and behind all the vowels: ab, ba, ec, ce, di, id, fo, of, gu, ug, etc. I then followed up with three letters: bud, dub, bic, cib, fag, gaf, goh, hog.[11]

From these three-letter combinations Pestalozzi moved on to ones of four and five letters and finally he built up long words (e.g. mu, muni, munici, municipal, municipality), which he found the children could read remarkably easily. Compared to modern methods of teaching reading, the success is perhaps surprising. One should, however, bear in mind that German spelling is much more consistent with pronunciation than English and also that any new method when taught with enthusiasm is likely to achieve a measure of success. The way in which Pestalozzi sometimes broke down topics into elements can sometimes, as here, be criticized for being overdone. It might be said of a mosaic that the smaller the stones, the easier it will be to fit them together to form an expressive picture or pattern – but it is equally true that if the stones were to become too small, they would become much more difficult to handle and the work would take too long. Thus the criticism should not invalidate the advantages of seeking out the elements, but indicate that to find the elements the topic does not necessarily have to be broken down into the smallest conceivable parts. After all Pestalozzi himself rejected teaching spelling and reading by going through the alphabet from beginning to end (i.e. individual letter by individual letter). Language work continued from reading to writing, where at first very few letters were taught, but these were immediately combined to form words with the result that the child could write many words before knowing even half the alphabet. There followed exercises to increase the vocabulary and others showing how sentences could be built up. Sometimes, as in the case of reading, the exercises became 'too' simple and thereby lost, rather than gained meaning. Girard and his fellow inspectors in their report did not fully approve of the text-books which were being used for language work in the Yverdon institute. On the other hand they acknowledged that language should form the basis of all education and hence they approved of the emphasis placed on language work.

Complete comprehension of the concepts of number and form were also an essential part of a child's intellectual education. Number helped to make him conscious of certain inner realities of the world around him. Through it he became conscious of quantity:

> The method develops the power of calculation not through a knowledge of mere figures, but through impressing deeply on the child the unit as the basis of all adding and all subtracting, and the area of the square as the basis of breaking down the unit.[12]

Through the concept of number the child was to gain understanding of positive and negative numbers and of fractions. Perception of form would enable the child to become conscious of certain outer realities, above all of the relationships between objects. The teaching of form was to be based on the straight and curved line in all its manifestations.

Initial experience of the two concepts should be gained through the senses, and if made aware of the world around him by his mother, the young child should already be conscious of quantity, distance, and shape before going to school. Once in school, exercises of increasing difficulty were to be devised. Thanks to Joseph Schmid such arithmetic exercises were used in Yverdon. Their aim was to avoid the rote learning of multiplication tables, mechanical calculations involving money, weights, and measures, and to concentrate on the mental processes involved in arithmetic. The children had to be taught to understand what they were doing. Sharply Pestalozzi attacked contemporary teaching of mathematics:

> But say how you feel when, at the public examination of a school which considers itself well above the average, you realize that children, who complete the most complicated commercial calculations, have not the slightest grasp of the most elementary relationships between numbers. Or say how you feel when those who explain difficult mathematical problems as if some higher spirit were speaking through them and as if the secrets of nature were in the process of being revealed to them, are faced with some small condition which has not been accounted for in the examples drummed into them and are therefore unable to see immediately whether

> the necessary proof is based on the seventh or eleventh principle – and then they stand there without powers of observation, without freedom, without the courage to help themselves, like butter in the sun.[13]

Pestalozzi hoped to put an end to mere 'juggling with formulae' and substitute a real, inner understanding of the principles involved in mathematics.

Form Pestalozzi regarded as the basis of writing, geometry, and drawing – those subjects for which close co-ordination between hand and eye were necessary. By 1806 Pestalozzi was satisfied with the progress which had been made:

> The scheme for teaching form and the relationships between forms which is a basis of both geometry and drawing has reached a stage of development and a degree of unity which we would not have considered feasible even a year ago. Every single one of us here, right down to the five year old child, does his exercises with the greatest interest.[14]

Mathematics was the subject which was most developed at Yverdon. Pestalozzi claimed that its teaching was more educative and more complete than it was anywhere else. The Girard report, while admitting Schmid's talent, accused the mathematics course in the institute of being insufficiently practical and of being given too large a place in the curriculum. It also said that the exercises were far from perfect. The latter criticism was undoubtedly justified – but only in the same way that criticism of some of the language exercises can be justified. There was a tendency to break down mathematical problems into so many different operations that they were thereby made more complicated rather than simpler. This was not Pestalozzi's intention. His aim, like that of those advocating the present revolutionary changes in mathematics teaching, was to make children abandon mechanical methods of solving problems and to teach them the basic principles involved.

The actual subjects in the timetable at Yverdon were conventional. Through his method Pestalozzi had attempted to show the links between subjects, establish a progression from simple to difficult in accordance with child psychology, and to emphasize mental training rather than knowledge of facts. Advocating the need for the child to proceed at his own pace and recognizing that the ability of children could vary considerably, it was natural that Pestalozzi should advocate the setting of pupils according to their ability:

> We try to ensure that the genius finds an open and sure path for his progress while the boy of average intelligence will be held back and thoroughly practised in that which he is learning as long as is necessary to ensure his progress . . . and to save him from superficial knowledge.[15]

At Yverdon Pestalozzi tried to introduce flexibility and meaning into a fairly conventional timetable. He hoped, however, to go further:

> There is no pupil who is capable of comprehending everything; equally there is none who does not enjoy one subject in particular and who would be unable, if he could apply himself sufficiently to it, to achieve excellence in it. The one fully enjoys number and form and shows indifference to everything else. Another devotes himself with enthusiasm and ease to language. A third takes up artistic subjects in particular, and draws very beautiful figures while remaining behind in other subjects. Others appear to be equally receptive to all subjects but to need variety to encourage them, and therefore these study everything with the same cheerfulness. The right moment to start a subject also varies and suddenly a pupil gains a new understanding for a subject which had previously been of no interest to him. Might not this be a sign of nature and might not an enormous amount be gained if, instead of teaching children in many subjects at once, one only did so until a particular preference became apparent, and then satisfied this yearning until through this one subject the need and the desire to learn another awoke in them.[16]

Pestalozzi accepted that there was a minimum general education which all pupils should be given, but still maintained that the instruction should be given at that point in time when a pupil felt naturally inclined to receive it. He does not give details of whether teachers should stimulate the inclination, or merely wait for it to appear, but he did recognize that the plan would involve changing traditional views on the purpose of education as well as considerable organizational difficulties. However practical or impractical the plan – and

Pestalozzi realized it was controversial – it is exemplary of Pestalozzi's desire to adapt education to the child.

Would it ever be possible to develop the ideal system of education as outlined by Pestalozzi? No, it would not. Every system of education will finally prove inadequate and piecemeal – but by presenting an ideal which strove after an education of the whole personality while insisting on the adaptation of educational material to the inborn needs and capacities of the child, Pestalozzi challenged the society of his day, as he does ours, to examine both the aims and methods of education and to reject all preconceived notions of both.

10 · Moral Education

So far we have treated the intellectual, moral, and practical aspects of education, as if they were three equal parts of a whole. Turning to Pestalozzi's views on moral education, it is necessary to readjust, but not contradict, this approach. Moral education, like the others, would be based on a series of experiences which proceed from the simple to the complex. Similarly, it should combine with intellectual and practical education to develop the child into a fully balanced individual. Yet, whereas the three forms of education were essential if a child's full potential as a human being were to be realized, Pestalozzi regarded moral education as being the most important, for, without it, the other types would lose their sense of direction:

> The ultimate goal of intellectual education and all its methods, the ultimate goal of all instruction, is to eradicate in man their original one-sidedness and limitations, and together to lose themselves in the unfathomable strength of perfect love as the common goal of perfect human education. In order that they may do this all their methods must be firmly subordinated to moral education.[1]

Pestalozzi continued by explaining why moral education was of such fundamental importance:

> The subordination of intellectual education to moral education follows on directly from the recognition of the basic aim of education: the elevation of ourselves to a sense of the inner dignity of our nature, and of the pure, higher, godly being, which lies within us. This sense is not developed by the power of our mind in thought, but is developed by the power of our heart in love.[2]

Pestalozzi stressed the humanizing element in Christianity. Awareness of God's love for man should give him a sense of security and should encourage his human virtues. However distorted, however repressed, there was within man an essential goodness, which separated him from all other living things:

> Man is good and seeks the good; his conscience only allows him to feel secure when he does the good; and if he is evil, it is surely because the way has been blocked, along which he wanted to be good. This blocking of the way is so terrible, and is yet so common – and man is therefore so seldom good. But nevertheless I have faith at all times, in every place, in the human heart, and in this faith I go along my rough road as if it were a fine Roman highway.[3]

Just as man was born with a seed of intellectual power within him, so, from his birth, he possessed the seed of human goodness. Above all else, it was the aim of education to nurture this seed, so that it would grow and flourish.

Pestalozzi set about examining the stages by which a child could attain a love of God – and through it the humanitarian virtues which he considered so important. He showed that not only was moral education more important than intellectual education, but that it started earlier. 'The child loves and believes', he wrote, 'before he thinks and acts.'[4] Indeed the moral education of a child started from the moment of his birth and centred around his relationship with his mother. At first a feeling of trust was created in him merely by the satisfaction of his physical needs:

> It is the ensured and quiet satisfaction of his physical needs which naturally stimulates and develops the first seeds of moral capacities in the baby from the moment of his birth. The sacred care of the mother, the attention which she instinctively pays to the immediate satisfaction of all his needs – needs which if not satisfied would be liable to upset him in a physically noticeable way – it is these which we must recognize as the first, but most essential, preparation and initiation for that state in which the first physical signs of trust towards the source of this satisfaction develop, and with them the first signs of love. It is in the stimulation of these first physical

manifestations of trust and love that the first physical manifestations of morality and religious feeling spring and develop.[5]

Pestalozzi traced a gradual progression in the child from the mere satisfaction of physical needs to feelings of trust, love, and gratitude for his mother. In time these feelings would be naturally extended to other human beings whom his mother liked or whom she resembled. Thus would be born in the child the first feelings of brotherly love.

Obedience developed in a similar fashion. The child was forced to be patient, and through patience to be obedient. At first patience and obedience were painful to the child, but eventually he learned that in making him obey her, his mother had his own interests in mind. The child would gradually become conscious that his mother was not in this world merely for his sake and thereby that he himself was not in this world merely to pursue his own interests. He would begin to conceive the meaning of duty and justice, i.e. the subordination of the self to human laws.

As intellectual education developed from an awareness of the outside world through the senses, so moral education developed from an awareness of the inner world through the heart. A child could never become aware of God and of God's love for man, until he had had experience of the human virtues of love, faith, trust, and obedience. And such experience could not be gained through any form of teaching – it had to be felt. For this reason the relationship between mother and child was of fundamental importance, for only through it could the child become even remotely aware of the relationship between God and man:

> Moral education is nothing more than the simple development of the human will through the higher feelings of love, of gratitude, and of trust in the ideal of perfection as these feelings reveal themselves in their first emergence from the pure relationship between mother and child. The aim of this education is perfection in thinking, feeling, and action. Visibly it reveals itself as morality in action (physical), invisibly as religion in feeling or meditation (spiritual). In the former it is the real, in the latter it is the ideal side of moral life which is being represented and which had one and the same starting point.[6]

Thus even before a child had gone to school he should have developed a trust in God, a feeling for human virtues, and a desire to serve his fellow-men.

When a child arrived at school the most important years of his life as far as moral education was concerned were already over. However, much could be done even at school as long as the right approach were adopted. The children should not be taught about religion and virtue, but instead they should be encouraged to lead a virtuous life. Even at Stans, Pestalozzi found he could achieve much by appealing directly to the moral sense of the children:

> At every occurrence in the house I turned to them and to this sense. Mostly at some quiet moment during the evening I asked them for their free judgement. When, for instance, it was said in the village that they did not get enough to eat, I said to them: 'Children, tell me, are you not better nourished than you were at home? Think it over and answer me: would it also be good if you were nourished in such a way that later you could not even by hard work and toil afford to buy and pay for the food you had become accustomed to eat daily? Tell me, do you think I could reasonably do more for you for the same expense? Would you yourselves wish that, with the money which I have, I maintained only 30 or 40 children instead of the 70 or 80 which you see that I now maintain, would that be right?'[7]

If the children misbehaved Pestalozzi made a similar direct appeal to them, by showing them the harm both to themselves and to others which their behaviour was liable to cause. For such an appeal to be successful, the spirit in which it was made was all-important. The children would only pay attention to someone for whom they had genuine affection. At Stans, Pestalozzi's questions and requests to the child were put as a father rather than as a teacher. The institutes at Burgdorf and Yverdon too, Pestalozzi conceived of as large families in which the teachers took over the role of the parents in encouraging family virtues. The children came to feel what was right and wrong, and developed a sense of responsibility towards the teachers and the other children.

Beside the attempts to impart moral education by seizing every informal opportunity to give the children experience of moral values, there was at Burgdorf and Yverdon more traditional religious instruction. At first the attention of pupils was drawn to their surroundings and to the circumstances of their life, and the presence of the divine in the world intimated. Then the children were given the Bible. A study of the Old Testament followed and the course was completed by one of the New Testament which was to show how Christianity had emerged. Every day there were prayers in the morning and evening, and on Sunday morning the children went to a church service. Every Sunday evening there was an assembly at which:

> the father of the house surveys the previous week, praises progress that has been achieved and good behaviour, alludes to mistakes which have been made and admonishes the perpetrators to improve. If this does not suffice, the culpable child must appear alone before Pestalozzi and the oldest teachers. This . . . is said to be the harshest punishment.[8]

Those wishing to do damage to Pestalozzi's cause accused him of neglecting proper religious instruction. It is, therefore, surprising to discover that Girard was so impressed by what he saw that he could write:

> The children in the institute find themselves under wise and good guidance. Indeed we can say that the moral discipline is the most complete, well developed, and excellent aspect of all the education in the institute. Heart and reason work together and what these undertake in harmony is the most likely to succeed. Benevolent attention has been shown to avoid anything which could frighten, embitter, or spoil the children and thereby the first duty of education has been fulfilled. . . .[9]

Pestalozzi intended to develop methods of teaching moral education as comprehensive as those used in intellectual education. Although he never managed to do so, moral education was always regarded as the centre of all education.

Pestalozzi was an educator, interested in the problems of society and the individual, and not a theologian interested in questions of doctrine. It was, therefore, natural that he should place emphasis on morality rather than religion. However, he believed that more could be achieved to establish both in the child's heart before he ever went to school, and in any case he regarded true religion as unobtainable if it did not grow out of human virtues. Just as a child had to learn to use the senses and express himself precisely before he could comprehend any intellectual concept, so he could never understand religion until he had learnt to use the language of morality. The language of morality could not be taught by word of mouth; it had to be taught by example. Practice, not preaching, was the basis of moral education.

11 · Physical Education

In Pestalozzi's system of total education the development of the body had great importance. The aim of gymnastic exercises 'is to bring back the body of the child into the full unity and harmony with his intellect and heart which originally existed'.[1] Only if a child developed his mental, moral, and physical capacities simultaneously could he reach the summit of his powers, for not only were the three capacities of importance in themselves, but also each stimulated and guided the experiences of the other two.

Pestalozzi vigorously attacked the neglect into which physical education had fallen. At least the wealthier sections of society enjoyed the leisure time and the food which could enable them to become physically active. Yet all too often they practised one physical skill to the neglect of all others:

> Nothing is more common in higher society than the dancer who cannot even walk properly, equestrians who cannot swim, fencers who cannot fell a tree with an axe. . . .[2]

The poor were in an even worse state and were rapidly becoming physical cripples. To some extent they could not help it; to stay alive required a solid day's work and even the children were often taken away from school to be engaged in a remunerative employment. Existence was a struggle and even health had to be sacrificed to it. Pestalozzi felt that the very narrowness of their lives aggravated their situation, for it induced in them a blindness to the dangers of ill-health and to the short-sightedness of their habit of forcing their children to enter some trade at a tender age. Physical exercise began to be looked down on as frivolous and time-wasting. Yet, Pestalozzi pointed out, this very emphasis on earning money was defeating its own ends. Neglect of physical fitness caused illness and premature old-age, and thereby restricted the capacity to earn a living. To allow children to enter a trade too early was extremely foolish, because if, after working at it for several years, they became redundant, they would be unable to adapt themselves to other forms of work.

And were the schools doing anything to counteract these deplorable tendencies, asked Pestalozzi.

> Yes – inasmuch as children have to walk to school and back home again, they are allowed to move, but in school itself they are barely allowed to twitch. That which is being done for their minds is given such unnatural importance that if a child so much as moves its hands and feet it forces the poor schoolmaster off the rails.[3]

The schools for the poor did not regard physical training as a necessary part of their syllabus. To teach poor children more than the bare minimum of knowledge would have been to give them ideas above their station. To indulge in physical exercises and sporting activities would have been irresponsible in the extreme.

Pestalozzi's proposals for remedying the state of affairs followed the general principles of the 'method'. Children had a natural urge to move. From the moment a child was born he made experiments with his body:

> His hand grasps after everything; he puts everything into his mouth. His feet are in continual motion. He plays with himself. He plays with everything. He throws everything away, just as he tries to seize everything.[4]

These simple movements form the foundation for all physical movement, and therefore it is the duty of the parents to encourage the physical activities of the child. Through them the child not only develops his physique, but also learns to pay attention to the outside world and to examine his relationship with his surroundings. Thus initially physical experiences give rise to mental and spiritual ones. As the child grows older and becomes less dependent on his parents, the school should try to widen the range of a child's muscular activities – while retaining the natural harmony between the physical, mental, and spiritual. A wide range of gymnastic exercises and games of increasing difficulty should build up the flexibility, strength, and agility of all a child's muscles, so that as an adult he can easily adapt himself to any form of physical exercise.

What is the ideal goal of physical education? Apart from physical qualities it should develop the primarily moral qualities of perseverance and courage. The child should learn control over himself, and begin to comprehend mentally his own physical powers and their limitations. Particular skills such as dancing and fencing will not only prepare the child for adult life, but will teach him something of the beauty of movement. Finally, the body should be capable of undertaking all the tasks which the child's future profession and station in life might demand of it.

In Yverdon there was no expert to work out a series of gymnastic exercises progressing from the simple to the difficult as there had been for a few of the academic subjects. Some exercises were devised for developing each joint and muscle in turn. Girard in his report described what was involved:

> The institute pays special attention to physical exercise and has also established its own elementary gymnastics according to certain principles. They begin with the head which the boys move in various directions; then, in order, come the arms, the feet, and finally the whole body. The essential aim here is to proceed from the simplest movements to the most complicated without missing any out.[5]

The report went on to state that the exercises were rather petty, especially for boys who were physically fit when they arrived at the institute. Even if the exercises were not satisfactorily devised, Pestalozzi could point to the good health of his pupils:

> The healthy state of our pupils and their on the whole vigorous appearance is certainly exceptional and striking to everyone. . . . Illnesses are very rare and many boys who were weakly when they arrived have recovered in a most impressive way.[6]

Pestalozzi attributed the health of the pupils firstly to cleanliness: the boys had to wash and comb their hair daily and received clean clothes regularly. Secondly, the school day at Yverdon provided a variety of occupations but regular hours and meals. Finally, there was plenty of opportunity for exercise (quite apart from the gymnastics). Between lunch and afternoon school and between half past three and five o'clock (in Summer between six and eight o'clock) the children were taken for walks in the summer and sledging or skating in the winter. Pestalozzi praised skating because

> it develops the deportment of the child in an excellent way; it makes him agile, courageous, and has, above all, the advantage that it increases immensely the children's desire, even in the hardest winter, to be in the open air and to enjoy its healthy effects.[7]

There were also dancing and fencing lessons for children whose parents desired it. In 1807 Pestalozzi decided to replace dancing by military drill when it was too hot for the former. With this wide variety of activity it is not surprising that even the Girard report, which did not treat Pestalozzi particularly sympathetically, had to corroborate his evidence on the physical fitness of the children:

> In the institute one sees on the whole a thriving youth, that cannot be denied; illnesses are rare there and do not last long; the children always appear cheerful.[8]

12 · Discipline

While attacking the old teaching methods which too often involved forcing knowledge into recalcitrant pupils by abundant use of the cane, Pestalozzi remained in favour of maintaining firm discipline in class. He never advocated any 'learn while you play' schemes: on the contrary he believed in the value of hard work. 'As for your principle', he wrote in one letter, 'that one should make children work hard and that good instruction is indeed only to be achieved through hard work, I am in entire agreement with you.'[1] Pestalozzi expected the teachers to stimulate the children's interest sufficiently to absorb them in the work being undertaken, and thereby avoid the necessity of imposing discipline by external means.

In order to learn their lessons properly, children must be protected from all unnecessary distractions. This was a lesson Pestalozzi learnt early, for he wrote of the home in Stans:

> Silence as a means of inducing activity is the first secret of such a home. The silence which I demanded when I was there and was teaching helped me greatly to achieve my aim as did my insistence on pupils sitting up properly. By the silence I made it possible on those occasions when I demanded all the children to repeat after me to hear every mispronunciation, and furthermore it enabled me to teach even with a soft, hoarse voice, not a word being heard other than that which I spoke and which the children had to repeat.[2]

Pestalozzi did not only believe that maintaining order in class helped the children to concentrate, but also claimed that the children learnt self-discipline by keeping quiet:

> An unruly girl who simply gets accustomed to sit up straight and hold her head up for hour after hour and not to let her eyes wander makes a degree of progress in moral education which none could credit who has not experienced it.[3]

If regular habits and good manners were instilled in the children, if the teachers presented their material in a fascinating way, then punishment would rarely be necessary. On those occasions when it could not be avoided, Pestalozzi considered corporal punishment justified as long as the relationship between the teacher and pupil was such that the pupil would understand, and therefore not resent his punishment. At Stans, Pestalozzi had found it necessary and effective:

> In view of the different backgrounds from which my beggar children came, in view of their age, their deeply engrained habits, the need in a simple way to make an impression on them all swiftly and surely, and the need to achieve one's aim with all of them, the effect of corporal punishment was considerable. The fear that one may thereby lose the trust of the children is quite unjustified. It is not single, rare actions which determine the feelings and attitude of the children; it is the true nature of your disposition towards them as revealed daily and hourly to them, and the degree to which you like or dislike them which fix once and for all their feelings towards you. This done, the impression created by individual actions will be interpreted according to the firm judgement of these inner feelings.[4]

In Yverdon Pestalozzi still maintained the same view:

> I am firmly against the striking of a strange pupil by a strange teacher, but not against a similar punishment by a father or mother. There are occasions when corporal punishment is undoubtedly the best thing; but it must be carried out with the greatest assurance from a parental heart, and the teacher who really reaches the point where he can act in the same spirit as a father or mother should have the right to act as they do in certain important cases which demand such measures.[5]

Pestalozzi recognized that teachers might sometimes abuse their right to use corporal punishment and punish more to satisfy their annoyance than to correct the child, and therefore the teachers at Yverdon were forbidden to give such punishment.

While considering forms of punishment, it is perhaps worth mentioning an interesting incident with his own son, which Pestalozzi describes:

> I took one of his nuts in order to crack it for him; he thought I wanted to eat it – he cried out, stamped, and pulled a face. I looked at him calmly. Without a word I took another and coldly ate both before his eyes. He went on crying; I took the mirror and he ran away, as usual, to hide himself.[6]

In his theoretical writings Pestalozzi never advocated this method of disciplining a child by putting him to shame; perhaps he found it inadequate, or detrimental to the relationship between teacher and child. In *Lienhard and Gertrud* the schoolmaster employed by the social reformer Arner maintained discipline simply by rebuking the disobedient children and by making them conscious that they were temporarily out of favour; and at Yverdon Pestalozzi himself seems to have found such methods usually sufficient, although he did reserve for himself the right to use corporal punishment.

Pestalozzi gave one important caution which applied to all punishments. It is essential that a child has a clear idea of what is right and what is wrong. Adults should not assume that a child knows this by instinct. For to punish a child who is innocent, or who really believes himself innocent, will create resentment within him and the teacher will lose his trust.

Corporal punishment was common in eighteenth-century schools. It was in no way reserved for grave misdemeanours but was used as a means of correcting mistakes made in class. Even a man like Dr Johnson could be a strong supporter of it:

> Children, being not reasonable, can only be governed by fear. To impress this fear, is therefore one of the first duties of those who have the care of children.[7]

As for himself, he claimed that he would have done nothing at school if his master had not 'whipt me very well'.[8] Pestalozzi's views on punishment opposed a widely held belief that both behaviour and intellect could be improved by flogging. By stressing that only teachers who knew the child's character intimately were in a position to punish him, Pestalozzi showed that punishment should be personal, and have positive effects. Often punishment would be avoided simply by better teaching; if not, it had to be administered justly, and for the child ignorance of the law was an adequate excuse. Whereas, in contrast to the eighteenth-century attitude to discipline, it is Pestalozzi's appeal for love and justice which most stands out, it should not be forgotten that he laid great importance on order in the class-room and acknowledged that even corporal punishment, if given in the right spirit, could have beneficial results. The attitude to discipline has always fluctuated between one of severity, often too harsh, and lenience, often too blind. Pestalozzi set out to compromise between the two extremes, not in a haphazard way, but on rational grounds. He saw corporal punishment neither as a cure of all evils nor as a form of punishment for which any substitute was a good one. In matters of discipline, as in other aspects of education, it was the interests of the child himself which Pestalozzi most had at heart.

13 · Parents and Teachers

'The first moment of a child's education is the moment of his birth'[1] – Pestalozzi can hardly have made a simpler, yet more important, statement. Rightly he did not separate off school education, i.e. formal education, as the sole realm of the educator, but saw every day in a child's life, every source of influence, as helping to form the child's character and personality. It naturally followed that the first years of a child's life, spent in the home, were as essential a part of his education as his years at school – indeed they were more so, for it was during infancy that the foundation was laid, upon which all school education would have to be built. The first environment in which the new-born child found himself, the home, and the first contacts he made with other people, his relationship with his parents, could, if properly cultivated, help to develop well-adjusted, lively, and happy children; on the other hand, if they were neglected, a child might become self-centred, suspicious, and unsettled.

Pestalozzi saw the ideal home as having a dual function. Firstly, it protected the child from the outside world; in it he would feel secure and would be sheltered from detrimental influences and empty knowledge. And secondly, it would stimulate him and provide the simple, but wholly adequate background for his moral, intellectual, and physical development:

> There can be no doubt that within the living-room of every household are united the essential basic elements of all true human education in its whole range.[2]

As Pestalozzi insisted that a child could only learn through his own experience and not through receiving second-hand knowledge from others, it was only the home which, at least during the earliest years of a child's life, could provide the sights and events and feelings necessary for a child's education – for the home, after all, contained the whole of a child's inward and outward experience.

To the very young child, his home was his world. At the centre of this world was his mother. It was her feelings, her beliefs, her actions, which the child would imitate; it was she, upon whom he depended for nourishment, for affection, and for life itself. The child's relationship with his mother conditioned all his other relationships – with the other members of his family, with his fellow-men, and ultimately with God Himself. Nowhere was the mother's careful guidance so influential as in the field of moral education. However, in intellectual and physical education too, the mother could play a vital role. The art of education lay in the selection and channelling of experiences:

> All human instruction is no more than the art of aiding nature in her forceful search for her own development, and this art is primarily based on the relation and harmony between the impressions to be made on the child and the specific stage which his developing powers have reached.[3]

When the child was very young, his mother was able to teach him instinctively:

> Indeed the existence and the unity of the method reveals itself nowhere so purely and so sublimely as in the way either the completely trained mother or the quite simple, natural mother treats her baby. Her treatment is elemental, it is distorted by no human artifice, by no human confusion. It is fundamental; in it nature expresses her whole self. . . .[4]

By instinct the mother should be able to present experiences to the child in such a way that he can comprehend them. She should steer the dangerous course between satisfying the basic needs of her child and over-indulging them. By talking to him she would begin the language teaching which was essential to all intellectual education; she would draw his attention to his surroundings and help him to systematize his sense impressions, thereby introducing him to the concepts of form and number. By playing with the child, first the mother, then the father, would begin to develop the child's physical capacities. If during the initial stages of education, whether intellectual, moral, or physical, parents could rely on instinct to show them the correct approach, they would, as their child became more mature and versatile, benefit from studying the principles of Pestalozzi's method. He hoped that his teaching method would not only help teachers, but also parents, to become more perceptive and articulate, and that parents too would make a conscious effort to heed the patterns along which their child's mind, body, and heart naturally developed.

Pestalozzi saw parents as teachers. He also saw teachers as parents, as the following description of the Burgdorf institute makes clear:

> Our house had, in order to attain its aims, to become a place of fatherly education, rather than one of public instruction. Cheerfulness, child-like devotion, open trust, refuge in the arms of the teacher as in the mother's arms, and the training of all forms of obedience, of perseverance, and of self-control to be achieved in their cheerfulness and through their devotion: on these we wished to lay the foundation of our house – in contrast to the opinion of the world which at present judges every educational institution primarily on the results of its instructional methods.[5]

Many teachers were in their profession only because of their incapacity to do anything else; all too often they had neither the personal qualities to understand their pupils nor the necessary insight into the purpose of education. They were unable even to begin to grasp their subject. When asked, for instance, why a calculation should be worked out in such and such a way, they would answer:

> Because everyone does it like that, and otherwise the answer would not come out right.[6]

For Pestalozzi the person of the teacher held in his power no less than the success or failure of the children whom he taught – not only at school but throughout life:

> If in a locality the schoolmaster is a man of affection, of wisdom and of virtue, if he is a man really up to his profession, if he is trusted by young and old alike, if he esteems affection, order, and self-control more highly and strives after them more assiduously than any particular distinction in the field of knowledge and learning, if he

> is a man who, endowed with deep insight, can perceive what the child must one day become as a man, as a woman, and is able by his affection and strength to lead the child through his school to that which he must become, then the teacher will, by his activity, become the father of the village in the true sense; by this activity he steps into the place of the best father and of the best mother and continues on the job of education when the latter could proceed no further. Such a man can and will uplift the spirit of a whole village and develop the young people in his charge to powers and capacities, to a way of thinking and acting which, while they maintain and strengthen the most sacred and proven in the thoughts and morals of past ages and attempt to perfect them in accordance with the needs of the present, will create and ensure the well-being of the village for the centuries to come.[7]

School should not become a place where a child's interests and energies were stifled. On the contrary they had to be stimulated. The teacher, therefore, had to avoid imposing his attitudes and ideas on his pupils but had to encourage theirs. It was not 'restriction from outside' but 'expansion from within'[8] that was necessary. The teacher had to be like a gardener, carefully tending his young plants. Only with the teacher's interest and encouragement could the child fully grow and mature. The teacher found himself between the child and life itself: through him the child had to learn about the outside world and about himself. Education involved not the imposing of knowledge but the development of potential.

Pestalozzi drew the obvious conclusion: the profession of schoolmastering was one which was highly skilled, one which demanded integrity, understanding, and intelligence. It could not, and should not, continue to be content with the second best. The right sort of people did not unfortunately 'drop from the sky'.[9] They would have to be sought out and properly trained for their exacting work. The state would have to care about the education of those under its protection as strongly as a parent does for his own child. Then, and only then, would the profession be seen in its correct light. It was, after all, the most important, as well as the most difficult profession.[10]

Education was an art, not merely an occupation. By insisting that every moment of a child's life contributed to his education, Pestalozzi showed the importance of the parents in education; the child's whole development rested in their care during the most formative days of his life. Even today the influence of the first years of a child's life over his adult personality has often been underestimated, and psychiatrists have to remind us how a healthy mother–child relationship creates a sense of security in the child. Teachers, as well as parents, had to possess the human qualities of patience and understanding. Yet even these qualities were not enough. Parents and teachers had to be able to educate a child by presenting him with the right experiences at the right time. Pestalozzi demanded skills as well as qualities. Parents and teachers had to have some knowledge of child psychology, of how to analyse material, and of how to express themselves in such a way that children would be able to understand them clearly. By extending the whole range of education, Pestalozzi laid down a challenge to parents and teachers alike. Their task was infinitely more complex than they had imagined it.

14 · Industrial Education

How to apply his principles to industrial education was always a preoccupation of Pestalozzi. The reason for this preoccupation lay in its fusion of his educational interests on the one hand with his social concern for the poor on the other. His methods of teaching, while developed in middle-class institutions, were applicable to the education of the poor. Their aim was to develop the whole human being – an aim equally beneficial to all classes of society. Again and again Pestalozzi attempted to set up a pioneer institute for poor children which would elaborate the activities and exercises necessary to equip the poor child for his adult life in a manual job. At the beginning of his own life Pestalozzi had tried to set up a poor-school in the Neuhof. When finally in Burgdorf and Yverdon his educational ideas were attracting widespread attention, he again sought support for an institute for the poor. Although he received plenty of moral support, the necessary financial support was not forthcoming. While he did manage to subsidize a few poor children in the Yverdon institute he never succeeded in firmly establishing the institute specifically for the poor upon which he had set his heart. However, in the Autumn of 1818, after the departure of Niederer and so many of the most faithful teachers, Pestalozzi did open a poor institute at Clindy, which was but a short distance from Yverdon. It flourished for a short time, but the expense of running it finally made Pestalozzi combine the two institutes in the Yverdon castle. By this time Pestalozzi was already too old to maintain the discipline necessary in a co-educational school of children coming from very different home backgrounds, and, as we have already noted, the organization of the Yverdon institute gradually disintegrated, and with it Pestalozzi's hopes of radically changing the system of educating the poor.

Even if the Clindy institute never reached the degree of perfection necessary for it to become a model institution for poor children, Pestalozzi had already made clear what he expected of such an institute and why he considered industrial education of such importance. During the early part of his life he had become aware that the increasing mechanization of industry and agriculture was not improving the lot of the poor as might have been expected. On the contrary, they were prepared, for the sake of a few more pence, to put themselves at the mercy of the industrialists. The exploitation of the poor brought about the destruction of old domestic virtues and substituted for them an all-consuming materialism. Instead of leading a healthy life in a job which provided interest and variety, the new worker found himself going through the same motions time and time again, day after day. The monotony and narrowness of his work was transferred to his whole existence. At the same time industry ceased to be run as a 'family business'. The employer began to lose interest in his employees. They gradually became for him no more than a means of earning him money, nothing more than puppets. For Pestalozzi the poor had lost their humanity not only in the eyes of their employers, but in their inner selves.

Pestalozzi had no doubts as to how to prevent the moral, intellectual, and physical decadence of the poor:

> There is so much misery in the world which can be avoided by education, and this method of avoiding misery is without question better for the noble dignity of men than the pitiful giving of alms which is normally deemed sufficient.[1]

Education was infinitely preferable to charity because it enabled the poor to help themselves, and, more important, because only through it was there the hope of altering the attitude of the poor to their lives. It was necessary to change them inwardly, not merely to improve their external circumstances.

The education which the poor were to be given was to be based largely on Pestalozzi's general principles of education. The normal methods of teaching the poor were far too specialized, with the result that work became monotonous, and if ever workers had to change their employment they found it almost impossible to adapt themselves to a new trade. Their training, if they received any, was responsible for this:

> All the institutions for educating the poor, of which I have so far heard, fail in their purpose above all because it is easy to come to the view with regard to the education of the poor that a semi-education is good enough, whereas human nature demands a whole education. A half is worth nothing.[2]

Education which merely imparted instruction in a single skill did not deserve the name of education:

> Industrial education is not the education of a single miserable factory skill. The true, but as yet unproven, aim of industrial education is essentially nothing more than the application of the whole of human education to the specific task of earning a living, and can only be called true industrial education if it is based on the full experience and whole range of human education itself.[3]

Pestalozzi, therefore, decided that for industrial education to be effective it must be based on a wide general education – for in his view it should concern itself much more than previously with the personality of the worker. It was on a man's character and intelligence, and not on his purely physical skill, that his happiness, diligence, and adaptability depended.

Pestalozzi advocated the establishment of a poor institute in order that the necessary adaptation of his methods to industrial education could be made. Series of exercises could be developed to follow on from the ordinary exercises of general education; none of the three aspects of education – moral, intellectual, and physical – was to be neglected. If this could be achieved, the industrial worker would cease to be a machine and regain his humanity.

Pestalozzi's desire for an institute did not arise solely from a wish to experiment, but also from the realization that the very poverty of the poor might even handicap the 'natural' education which the simplest of parents were capable of giving their children. In an institute the staff should try to give as much time and attention to the children as possible, and thereby make good the inevitable inadequacies of the very poor home. In addition, the facilities of an organized institution should enable them to develop the children more fully than even the best-placed poor parents could hope to achieve:

> In such an institute the opportunities to develop the physical, intellectual, and moral powers are much more easily available, more comprehensive, and can more easily penetrate into the deeper aspects of human nature and action than would be possible in the limited confines of a household struggling against hardship and poverty.[4]

The conditions in which some of the poor lived were so abject that home life ceased to be a source of education and encouragement for their children. The children's potential was neglected; it was their very existence which was in the balance. Pestalozzi hoped that a model institute would not only investigate the technicalities of teaching the poor, but would be the first of a series of institutes to cater for those children who came from homes so poor that proper home education was not practicable.

In recommending a general system of education for the poor, Pestalozzi was involving himself in one of the most controversial issues of the time. There was no possibility of establishing poor education without the co-operation of the ruling classes; and the latter regarded any form of general education as a threat to their position of privilege. Before the French Revolution change was already in the air and was being fiercely resisted by the aristocracy; after 1789 the Revolution itself gave rise to so many brutalities that even those who had previously advocated change now spoke out against it. Pestalozzi took pains to state his view that the lot of the poor could only be improved gradually, and not through a radical change in social structure:

> Far from believing that one should lead the children of an institute for the poor outside the boundaries of their social position and conditions, I believe it an essential requirement that in it they be made continually conscious of their poverty and their real situation and that they be forced to accept all the exertions and efforts peculiar to their class.[5]

Many agreed that education necessarily produced in the poor dissatisfaction with their way of life. Pestalozzi denied this. Indeed he asserted the contrary: cunning and deception in the common people were signs of a lack of education, and certainly not valid reasons for not giving one. If a man's capacities were prevented from developing naturally, they would naturally follow a devious course. Pestalozzi did not compromise his desire for universal education, but sought to sever it from the social issue:

> The question: Is it good to channel the judgements and knowledge of the common people into matters which lie outside their social class, their position, and their needs? is a basically different question from the question: Is it in any way desirable to rouse the minds of men in all classes and to stimulate knowledge for its own sake?[6]

If only the education of the poor could be seen outside its social context, progress could be made in a more lasting and less violent way than had been achieved in the French Revolution. What was needed was a change in attitude, not a change in class. Through proper education the poor man would not wish to reject his manual skills, but would learn to render them more flexible, and, if necessary, to adapt them to various jobs; above all, he would gain a feeling of satisfaction with his work. It was self-reliance, self-confidence, and self-fulfilment which Pestalozzi hoped to achieve through education. The poor had as much right to these as anybody.

15 · Conclusion

Pestalozzi is an educational thinker who will always merit study because he emphasized those aspects of education which must always be emphasized. He acknowledged the essential, but neglected, place of education in society; he recognized the humanity of the child; and he stressed that every aspect of a child's life contributed to the formation of his personality. The child lived in his own conceptual and emotional world, and in order to be able to guide him, this world had to be the subject of infinite, painstaking study. It could never be fully understood, but the more that was uncovered about a child's development, the more effectively could teaching methods encourage the natural processes of growth. Pestalozzi's clear vision of the ultimate goals of education, combined with his flexibility of approach, make him an educational thinker who deserves to be read. The energy and directness of his style make him worth reading.

The world of today is very different from Pestalozzi's world. In America and Western Europe the process of industrialization has continued, life in the country has been largely superseded by life in the town, the pace of life has quickened, the family as a social unit has been weakened, work has become more mechanical and more monotonous, and the individual has to undergo mental stresses very different in degree and nature to those which would have afflicted him a century and a half ago. Colonialism, the development of world trade and of communications, and wars on a vast scale have caused the pressures and values of European and American civilization to be thrust on the other countries of the world. They are faced with altering their way of life while retaining their national identity. In these countries too the individual is being subjected to new and dangerous strains. Yet, with the changing world, Pestalozzi's assertions have become more, not less relevant. For by insisting that education began at birth, Pestalozzi recognized the influence of the first years of a child's life on his developing a balanced and healthy personality. During the very first months of life a sense of security should be established in the child, and on this depends his behaviour not only as a child but in adulthood too:

> The maintenance of a feeling of tranquillity and satisfaction in the baby child . . . is of fundamental importance for the emergence of his humanity.[1]

Recent research has not only confirmed Pestalozzi's belief in the educational importance of the first years of life, but has also underlined the role of the mother in creating the sense of security within her child. One expert has stressed that partial maternal deprivation:

> brings in its train acute anxiety, excessive need for love, powerful feelings of revenge, and, arising from these last, guilt and depression. . . . Complete deprivation . . . has even more far-reaching effects on character development and may entirely cripple the capacity to make relationships.[2]

At no other period of life can a child's lack of security have such widespread effect, for it can produce not only permanent emotional disturbance, but also mental retardation.

Acknowledging the influence of the mother–child relationship on the child's later personality makes it no easier to find the right formula for creating the desired sense of security within the child. Professor MacCalman has indicated both the confusion a mother must face through the wealth of 'expert' advice she is given, and the dependence of her approach on her own experiences as a child.[3] However difficult it may be to outline in detail the ideal method of bringing up a child, Pestalozzi stressed that it was the fundamental attitude of parents on which all depended:

> The serious abandonment by fathers and mothers of their belief in themselves is the basic cause of the lack of a real foundation for educational methods.[4]

In Pestalozzi's time new industries were already beginning to threaten family life. Nowadays the temptation for mothers to go out to work while their children are still at a tender age is even greater, and the factors of modern civilization tending to disrupt home life are more numerous. But even if it is impossible to prescribe infallible techniques for bringing up children well, there must be a firm belief by parents in the family as the basic social unit 'par excellence'.

It was a central aim of Pestalozzi to analyse all educational material, to reduce it to its simplest elements, and then to present it gradually to the child in such a way that the level of difficulty always corresponded to the child's capacity to comprehend it. Pestalozzi realized that to achieve this it was necessary on the one hand to learn far more about the child and the way in which his mind and personality developed, and on the other hand to relate this information to the knowledge and experiences with which one wished the child to become acquainted. Modern psychology is concerned with both these problems. Firstly, research into the physiology of the brain is attempting to explain the mechanical processes involved in cognition. Secondly, the preoccupation with methods of assessing and selecting individuals according to intelligence and aptitude has resulted in endeavours being made to isolate mental processes from the facts and ideas through which they necessarily reveal themselves. Pestalozzi searched for the 'elements' of human perception and claimed to have found them in language, number, and form. Modern psychologists are attempting to obtain a clearer idea of these elements and to show how they develop in children. The work of Piaget is exemplary. By examining various areas of a child's experience, e.g. language and speech, shape and size, Piaget has shown conclusively that a child's capacity to grasp certain concepts develops gradually through definite stages, and that therefore it is unreasonable to expect a child to understand and express thoughts in an adult way before he has passed through all the preliminary stages of development.

Piaget's work has been primarily in the field of pure research. Modern trends in the practical field of teaching are based on the same belief that there is an ideal order in which to present a subject to children. For instance, the presentation of both mathematics and science is gradually being changed so that pupils will no longer answer problems by automatically applying procedures and formulae which they have learnt by heart, but which they do not really understand. Instead they will have to think the answers out for themselves, often drawing on their experience of many aspects of the subject, often having to work out their own experiments. The teaching of other subjects too is being adapted to satisfy more fully the natural capacities of the child. In connexion with language teaching, much research has been done in word frequency, sentence structure, and phonetics; the fruits of this research are now being used in the writing of text-books and the recording of tapes, so that the most common and useful words are used before rarer ones and simple grammatical constructions precede the more complicated ones, with the ultimate result that, moving on from the basic elements, a practical and confident knowledge of a foreign language will be built up. The traditional methods of teaching religion and the mother-tongue are being questioned, and undoubtedly they also will be brought closer to the experience of the child. The teaching of all subjects is being influenced by modern technical advances. Pestalozzi's two principles that the simple should precede the difficult, and that the child should not continue to the second stage in any learning process before having mastered the first stage, find their modern application in teaching machines and programmed learning. Pestalozzi would also have approved of the use of modern audio-visual aids, as they are in accordance with his precept that instruction should be made through as many of the five senses as possible.

Although much progress has been made towards adapting individual subjects to the needs of the child, attitudes to education as a whole are often fettered by tradition. The subjects of a school curriculum have changed little since Pestalozzi's day, and increased specialization has tended to isolate them from each other. In addition, the subjects taught are far more adapted to the needs of the academic child than to those of the non-academic. The desire to prevent vocational education interfering with general education has all too often led to general education becoming divorced from life itself.

Pestalozzi was intensely conscious of the failure of the education of his day to prepare children both emotionally and intellectually for their life as adults. He knew that radical changes were necessary and proposed that:

G

> the carriage of European education should not merely be pulled along more surely but should be turned right around and taken on to a new road.[5]

Today, too, some basic rethinking about educational problems is necessary. In a world with a rapidly increasing population, of whom some sixty per cent can neither read nor write, it is essential to extend educational facilities so that all children will have the opportunity to develop their capacities to the full. Whatever their ability, through education they must be able to experience a sense of achievement and become aware of the contribution they can make to the community. Schools should prepare children for adult life in such a way that no one can claim, like Mark Twain, that he did not allow his schooling to interfere with his education. To solve the problems of modern education the vision and perseverance of Pestalozzi are needed, and much of his wisdom also.

Bibliography

There are three comprehensive editions of Pestalozzi's works:

1 *Pestalozzis sämtliche Schriften*, I. G. Cottasche Buchhandlung, Stuttgart and Tübingen, 1819–26.

2 *Pestalozzis sämtliche Werke*, 2nd edition, edited by L. W. Seyffarth, Liebnitz, 1899–1902.

3 *Pestalozzi. Sämtliche Werke*, edited by A. Buchenau, E. Spranger, and H. Stettbacher, Berlin, Leipzig, Zürich, 1927–.

The latter edition should prove the most complete and most accurate, but is unfortunately not yet available in entirety; there are still some of the planned twenty-seven volumes to appear.

There are also some good editions of selected works. Among these may be mentioned:

Heinrich Pestalozzi, Gesammelte Werke in zehn Bänden, edited by E. Bosshart, E. Dejung, L. Kempter, H. Stettbacher, Zürich, 1944–47 (10 vols.).

Heinrich Pestalozzi, Werke in acht Bänden. Gedenkausgabe zu seinem zweihundertsten Geburtstage, edited by P. Baumgartner, Rotapfel Verlag, Erlenbach-Zürich, 1945–49 (8 vols.).

Heinrich Pestalozzis lebendiges Werk, edited by A. Haller, Birkhäuser Verlag, Basel, 1946 (4 vols.).

Pestalozzi. Ausgewählte Schriften, 2nd edition, edited by W. Flitner, Verlag Helmut Küpper, Düsseldorf and Munich, 1954 (1 vol.).

Pestalozzi's letters are an excellent source of information about his life, and are in the process of appearing in a collected edition:

Johann Heinrich Pestalozzi. Sämtliche Briefe, Orell Füssli Verlag, Zürich 1946–.

A selection of letters in one volume can be found in:

Ausgewählte Briefe Pestalozzis, edited by H. Stettbacher, Verlag Benno Schwabe and Co., Basel, 1945.

Reminiscences of Pestalozzi by some of his contemporaries have been republished recently. These can, for example, be found in:

Pestalozzi im Lichte zweier Zeitgenossen: Henning und Niederer, postscript by E. Dejung, Zürich, 1944.

Pestalozzi im Urteil zweier Mitarbeiter: Krüsi und Niederer 1839–1840, annotated and introduced by E. Dejung, Zürich, 1961.

Begegnungen mit Pestalozzi. Ausgewählte zeitgenössische Berichte, edited by W. Klinke, Verlag Benno Schwabe and Co., Basel, 1945.

There are many books about Pestalozzi in German, but very few in English. A thorough account of his life and work can be found in:

Pestalozzi, the man and his work, by K. Silber, Routledge and Kegan Paul, London, 1960.

Notes

The references of the German quotations (translated by the author) have been given to the original German texts. In the case of Pestalozzi's works the references have been given, where possible, to the *Sämtliche Werke*; where this has not been possible they have been given to some other edition, usually the 8-volume edition published by the Rotapfel Verlag (volumes 4–8 of the edition are entitled *Schriften* and numbered 1–5). With each reference to Pestalozzi's works is added the title (often in abbreviated form) of the actual work from which the quotation was taken; this should give some help to readers with other editions. Details of books mentioned in the bibliography are not given in full here.

CHAPTER 1

1 Pestalozzi, *Schriften* 5 (1805–26), p. 426, 'Schwanengesang'
2 Frederick the Great, *L'histoire de mon temps*, reprinted in Vol. IV of the *Publikationen aus den K. Preuss. Staatsarchiven*, Leipzig, 1879, p. 198
3 Pestalozzi, *Schriften* 5 (1805–26, II), p. 440, 'Schwanengesang'
4 Rousseau, *Emile* (in preface)
5 Pestalozzi, *Schriften* 5 (1805–26, II), p. 440, 'Schwanengesang'
6 Ibid., p. 442
7 Pestalozzi, *Sämtliche Werke*, Vol. 14, p. 93, 'Selbstschilderung'
8 Pestalozzi, *Sämtliche Briefe*, Vol. 1, pp. 29–30

CHAPTER 2

1 Pestalozzi, *Sämtliche Werke*, Vol. 1, p. 137, 'Eine Bitte an Menschenfreunde und Gönner . . .'

2 Pestalozzi, *Sämtliche Werke*, Vol. 1, p. 143, 'Herrn Pestalotz Brief an Herrn N. E. T. über die Erziehung der armen Landjugend'
3 Ibid., p. 143
4 Ibid., p. 175
5 Pestalozzi, *Schriften* 5 (1805–26, II), p. 448, 'Schwanengesang'
6 Pestalozzi, *Sämtliche Werke*, Vol. 13, p. 183, 'Wie Gertrud ihre Kinder lehrt'

CHAPTER 3

1 Pestalozzi, *Schriften* 5 (1805–26, II), p. 451, 'Schwanengesang'
2 Pestalozzi, *Sämtliche Werke*, Vol. 13, p. 184, 'Wie Gertrud ihre Kinder lehrt'
3 Pestalozzi, *Sämtliche Werke*, Vol. 8, p. 242, 'Das Schweizerblatt', Band 2, No. 33, 15–8–1782
4 Pestalozzi, *Schriften* 5 (1805–26, II), p. 455, 'Schwanengesang'
5 Ibid., p. 456
6 Pestalozzi, *Sämtliche Briefe*, Vol. 3, p. 83
7 Pestalozzi, *Sämtliche Werke*, Vol. 13, p. 185, 'Wie Gertrud . . .'
8 Pestalozzi, *Sämtliche Briefe*, Vol. 3, p. 239
9 Ibid., Vol. 5, p. 251
10 Ibid., Vol. 3, p. 295
11 Ibid., Vol. 5, p. 201

CHAPTER 4

1 Pestalozzi, *Sämtliche Werke*, Vol. 13, p. 188, 'Wie Gertrud . . .'
2 Ibid., Vol. 13, pp. 9–10, 'Pestalozzis Brief an einen Freund über seinen Aufenthalt in Stans'
3 Ibid., p. 12
4 Ibid., p. 15
5 Pestalozzi, *Sämtliche Briefe*, Vol. 4, p. 20

CHAPTER 5

1 Pestalozzi, *Sämtliche Werke*, Vol. 13, p. 194, 'Wie Gertrud . . .'
2 Pestalozzi, *Sämtliche Briefe*, Vol. 4, p. 54

3 Ibid., p. 237
4 Ibid., p. 146
5 Ibid., p. 163
6 Pestalozzi, *Sämtliche Werke*, Vol. 13, p. 195, 'Wie Gertrud . . .'
7 Pestalozzi, *Schriften* 5 (1805–26, II), p. 472, 'Schwanengesang'
8 Pestalozzi, *Sämtliche Briefe*, Vol. 5, p. 21
9 *Pestalozzi im Urteil zweier Mitarbeiter: Krüsi und Niederer*, p. 69

CHAPTER 6

1 Pestalozzi, *Sämtliche Briefe*, Vol. 4, p. 21
2 Ibid., Vol. 6, p. 12
3 Ibid., Vol. 5, p. 258
4 *Pestalozzi im Urteil zweier Mitarbeiter: Krüsi und Niederer*, p. 82
5 Pestalozzi, *Sämtliche Briefe*, Vol. 6, p. 3
6 Ibid., Vol. 5, p. 143
7 Ibid., Vol. 5, p. 143
8 Passage from *Souvenirs racontés à ses petits enfants*, by L. Vulliemins, quoted in A. Haller, *Pestalozzis Leben in Briefen und Berichten*, Ebenhausen, 1927, p. 284
9 Ibid., p. 284
10 *Pestalozzi im Lichte zweier Zeitgenossen: Henning und Niederer*, p. 91
11 Pestalozzi, *Sämtliche Briefe*, Vol. 5, p. 205

CHAPTER 7

1 K. F. von Klöden, *Jugenderinnerungen*, Leipzig, 1911, pp. 69–70
2 Pestalozzi, *Sämtliche Briefe*, Vol. 3, p. 141
3 Pestalozzi, *Sämtliche Werke*, Vol. 13, p. 199, 'Wie Gertrud . . .'
4 Ibid., p. 198
5 Pestalozzi, *Sämtliche Briefe*, Vol. 4, p. 155
6 Ibid., p. 268
7 Pestalozzi, *Sämtliche Werke*, Vol. 20, p. 311, 'Über Unterrichts- und Erziehungs-Verbesserungen in Schulen und Haushaltungen, in Abendgesprächen zweyer Freunde'

CHAPTER 8

1 Pestalozzi, *Sämtliche Werke*, Vol. 13, p. 196, 'Wie Gertrud . . .'
2 Pestalozzi, *Schriften* 4 (1805–26, I), p. 199, 'Über die Idee der Elementarbildung' (Lenzburger Rede)
3 Ibid., p. 199
4 *Pestalozzi im Lichte zweier Zeitgenossen: Henning und Niederer*, pp. 70–1
5 Pestalozzi, *Sämtliche Werke*, Vol. 13, p. 245
6 Pestalozzi, *Schriften* 4 (1805–26, I), p. 168, 'Über die Idee der Elementarbildung'
7 Pestalozzi, *Sämtliche Werke*, Vol. 13, p. 247, 'Wie Gertrud . . .'
8 Ibid., Vol. 20, pp. 320–1, 'Über Unterrichts- und Erziehungs-Verbesserungen . . .'
9 Pestalozzi, *Schriften* 5 (1805–26, II), p. 259, 'Schwanengesang'
10 Ibid., 4 (1805–26, I), p. 174, 'Über die Idee der Elementarbildung'
11 Ibid., p. 133
12 Pestalozzi, *Ausgewählte Schriften*, ed. W. Flitner, p. 168, 'Bericht an die Eltern und an das Publikum über den Zustand und die Einrichtungen der Pestalozzischen Anstalt'
13 Pestalozzi, *Schriften* 4 (1805–26, I), p. 165, 'Über die Idee der Elementarbildung'

CHAPTER 9

1 Pestalozzi, *Sämtliche Werke*, Vol. 18, p. 31, 'Über Geist und Herz in der Methode'
2 Ibid., p. 38
3 Ibid., p. 18
4 Ibid., Vol. 13, pp. 194–5, 'Wie Gertrud . . .'
5 Pestalozzi, *Sämtliche Briefe*, Vol. 3, p. 142
6 Ibid., p. 131
7 Pestalozzi, *Sämtliche Werke*, Vol. 13, p. 198, 'Wie Gertrud . . .'
8 Pestalozzi, *Ausgewählte Schriften*, ed. W. Flitner, p. 180, 'Bericht an die Eltern . . .'
9 Ibid., p. 181
10 Pestalozzi, *Schriften* 4 (1805–26, I), p. 193, 'Über die Idee der Elementarbildung'

11 Pestalozzi, *Sämtliche Werke*, Vol. 13, p. 134, 'Pestalozzis Brief . . .über seinen Aufenthalt in Stans'
12 Pestalozzi, *Sämtliche Briefe*, Vol. 4, p. 107
13 Pestalozzi, *Sämtliche Werke*, Vol. 20, p. 323, 'Über Unterrichts- und Erziehungs-Verbesserungen'
14 Pestalozzi, *Sämtliche Briefe*, Vol. 5, p. 161
15 Pestalozzi, *Ausgewählte Schriften*, ed. W. Flitner, p. 178, 'Bericht an die Eltern . . .'
16 Ibid., p. 179

CHAPTER 10

1 Pestalozzi, *Sämtliche Werke*, Vol. 18, pp. 36–7, 'Über Geist und Herz in der Methode'
2 Ibid., p. 37
3 Ibid., Vol. 13, p. 244, 'Wie Gertrud . . .'
4 Pestalozzi, *Schriften* 5, (1805–26, II), p. 284, 'Schwanengesang'
5 Ibid., p. 260, 'Schwanengesang'
6 Ibid., 4, (1805–26, I), p. 185, 'Über die Idee der Elementarbildung'
7 Pestalozzi, *Sämtliche Werke*, Vol. 13, p. 20, 'Pestalozzis Brief . . . über seinen Aufenthalt in Stans'
8 *Bericht über die Pestalozzische Erziehungs-Anstalt zu Yverdon*, Bern 1810, p. 65
9 Ibid., p. 183

CHAPTER 11

1 Pestalozzi, *Sämtliche Schriften*, Vol. 20, p. 65, 'Über Körperbildung, als Einleitung auf den Versuch einer Elementargymnastik in einer Reihenfolge körperlicher Übungen'
2 Ibid., p. 48
3 Ibid., p. 52
4 Ibid., p. 58
5 *Bericht über die Pestalozzische Erziehungs-Anstalt zu Yverdon*, Bern 1810, p. 21
6 Pestalozzi, *Ausgewählte Schriften*, ed. W. Flitner, p. 180, 'Bericht an die Eltern . . .'
7 Pestalozzi, *Sämtliche Briefe*, Vol. 6, p. 25
8 *Bericht über die Pestalozzische Erziehungs-Anstalt zu Yverdon*, Bern 1810, p. 129

CHAPTER 12

1 Pestalozzi, *Sämtliche Briefe*, Vol. 5, p. 108.
2 Pestalozzi, *Sämtliche Werke*, Vol. 13, p. 17, 'Pestalozzis Brief . . . über seinen Aufenthalt in Stans'
3 Ibid., p. 17
4 Ibid., p. 18
5 Pestalozzi, *Sämtliche Briefe*, Vol. 6, p. 25
6 Pestalozzi, *Sämtliche Werke*, Vol. 1, p. 121, 'Tagebuch Pestalozzis über die Erziehung seines Sohnes'
7 J. Boswell, *The Life of Dr. Johnson*, Everyman's Library, London 1949, Vol. 1, p. 281
8 Ibid., p. 18

CHAPTER 13

1 Pestalozzi, *Sämtliche Werke*, Vol. 13, p. 196, 'Wie Gertrud . . .'
2 Pestalozzi, *Schriften* 4, (1805–26, I), p. 475, 'Rede an mein Haus', 1818
3 Pestalozzi, *Sämtliche Werke*, Vol. 13, p. 197, 'Wie Gertrud . . .'
4 Pestalozzi, *Schriften* 4 (1805–26, I), p. 182, 'Über die Idee der Elementarbildung'
5 Pestalozzi, *Sämtliche Werke*, Vol. 18, p. 30, 'Geist und Herz in der Methode'
6 Ibid., Vol. 20, p. 325, 'Über Unterrichts- und Erziehungs-Verbesserungen'
7 Ibid., Vol. 19, p. 75, 'Ansichten Erfahrungen und Mittel zur Beförderung einer der Menschennatur angemessenen Erziehungsweise'
8 Pestalozzi, *Schriften* 4 (1805–26), p. 173, 'Über die Idee der Elementarbildung'
9 Pestalozzi, *Sämtliche Werke*, Vol. 19, p. 77, 'Ansichten Erfahrungen . . .'
10 See ibid., p. 77

CHAPTER 14

1 Pestalozzi, *Sämtliche Briefe*, Vol. 5, p. 228
2 Pestalozzi, *Sämtliche Werke*, Vol. 20, p. 103, 'Mémoire über Armenversorgung mit spezieller Rücksicht auf Neuenburg'
3 Ibid., Vol. 18, p. 60, 'Zweck und Plan einer Armen-Erziehungs-Anstalt'
4 Ibid., p. 67

5 Ibid., Vol. 20, pp. 100–1, 'Mémoire über Armenversorgung . . .'
6 Ibid., Vol. 18, p. 189, 'Ein Gespräch über Volksaufklärung und Volksbildung'

CHAPTER 15

1 Pestalozzi, *Schriften* 5 (1805–26, II), p. 261, 'Schwanengesang'
2 J. Bowlby, *Maternal Care and Mental Health*, p. 12, World Health Organization, Geneva 1952
3 See D. R. MacCalman, 'Problems of early infancy', in *Researches and Studies* No. 13, Jan. 1956, The University of Leeds Institute of Education
4 Pestalozzi, *Schriften* 4 (1805–26, I), p. 456, 'Rede an mein Haus', 1818
5 Pestalozzi, *Sämtliche Werke*, Vol. 13, p. 319, 'Wie Gertrud . . .'

Index